SUCCEED
BIG
PROFESSIONALLY

MICHAEL G. DRAKE

Ron,
Thank you.

—Mike D

To Lindsey, for supporting me from the first mention of writing a book, the many hours spent proofing and editing (all remaining mistakes are my own), and for always making me smile.

To my brother, may you learn these lessons and be amazingly successful.

To my mother, father, and grandmother, with love and gratitude.

To Won Sun Jung, Albert O'Neil, Mark Weeks, & Mark Taylor, with honor and respect.

To Ron & Ron at Acadia, & Jan for their ongoing professional support and guidance.

To my team at Acadia, the living test box for the successful management practices you read about in this book, and the failed management practices not included here.

To those whom I have loved and lost.

Contents

Introduction

"Luck is what happens when preparation meets opportunity".
- Seneca

How is it that some people seem to be so lucky in their professional lives? They work in a job that fulfills them personally and financially, they receive regular opportunities for advancement, and they seem to be truly happy. These types of people exist in every profession in the world. Do they share traits in common that make them successful, or are they just lucky?

Almost all successful people just seem to be lucky. Their luck actually stems from practicing certain methods and philosophies that help them prepare for good opportunities, in addition to strengthening the tools to create their own.

Succeed Big Professionally isn't about any single type of career, but instead a guide to professional success that anyone can apply, in any industry. Whether you begin your career at a start-up, Fortune 500 Corporation, or non-profit foundation, there are certain near-universal approaches to success.

An early working title of this book was "The First Ten Years." That title is instructive in understanding some of the key themes herein. While you can enjoy strong professional growth and success later in life, many of those opportunities come from the experience, achievements, and reputation that you build in the first stages of your career. The first ten years are when you can really create a foundation of positive development and momentum, opening up many possibilities for your future. When you capitalize on those possibilities and succeed…most people would call that luck.

The start of Summer 2014 marked the ten-year point since my high school graduation. That is a long time! At least I think so. So much can change in a single year, let alone ten of them. To any high school or college-aged reader, I'm already an old man.

There have been more highs and lows for me in these past ten years than many people have in their entire careers. Within this period, I've learned many lessons about professional success. Some of these lessons have been very costly, both professionally and personally. Where I am today is certainly not the picture I had as a graduating senior in high school. That isn't good or bad; life is exciting in part because of its unpredictability. By giving yourself as many opportunities as possible, you will have a journey that you would or could never expect or plan for.

My professional career began with start-ups and small companies. The practices here apply as much to a company of ten people as one with ten-thousand people. Success in a company, large or small, relies on being a valuable part of the team when you are an employee, and on creating a valuable strategy and team when you are a manager.

I learned many of these concepts because I always wanted to run my own business, which requires a holistic understanding of all areas: finance, sales and marketing, operations, human resources, etc. When I moved from a small company to one with twenty-thousand employees, I realized those skills are just as applicable in either scenario. Don't get me wrong, I'm not saying a ten-person company is the same as one with ten-thousand employees, but I do think there are many elements that translate. In this day and age of rapid change, larger companies have to think and act more like smaller companies to meet the needs of their customers and harness new opportunities that emerge.

Understanding what these opportunities look like and being prepared to leverage them is crucial. Certain opportunities come only once every few years, if not once in a lifetime. The opportunities you seize in the first ten years of your professional life will set the trajectory of your career. Make them count.

What's Inside

Succeed Big Professionally is laid out with the idea of showcasing the skills and methodologies that are common to professional success. Every concept here has been or is currently applied in practice, not in theory. Meant to be a comprehensive guide, the book goes from basic to more advanced concepts in (roughly) consecutive order. If any one chapter feels apparent, skip to the next one.

Part One focuses on being a great member of and contributor to an organization to advance your career. First in selecting and applying to the right job in an organization, then maximizing your chances to do well within that organization.

Part Two addresses what it takes to be a great manager, namely by developing and executing strategy, as well as building and leading teams to exceptional outcomes. If you are a manager (or about to be), you may wish to start with Part Two.

These first two parts are analogues to one another. A benefit of writing this book now is that I still remember everything required to be a great contributor, and I have been managing long enough to have developed a strong framework for leading teams.

Part Three is my own story, so far, which explains how those lessons were learned.

If you read every page and feel that you not only understand everything, but already actively do all of these things, contact me. You are likely an awesome person who I would like to get to know.

May you succeed big professionally. - MD

Part One: Building a Successful Career

Section One: Choosing a Career Path That Fits

Show me any profession in the world and I will show you a success story. Blue collar, white collar, no collar, every type of work has a certain number of people who live happy, fulfilling, and successful lives. Perhaps more bankers live affluently, and perhaps more tour guides have fun day-to-day, but every and any job can result in success.

History is full of those who started with nothing and ended up with everything. Many millionaires began their careers as taxi drivers. Twenty years ago, cooking wasn't considered a prestigious profession; today, a talented chef is a rock star. While some jobs may make that path harder or longer, success can be achieved in all of them.

What is success? Everyone has a different definition. For some, success means being a millionaire or having the money to buy whatever they wish. For others, it is means providing a stable life for them and their families, or doing well enough to be able to pursue a passion, full-time or part-time. Success may be equated with fame or notoriety. Success might mean being the best in your profession, however grand or not it may be. What is your definition of success? Create your definition and seek out a career that achieves it.

Chapter 1: What Drives You?

Some people know exactly what they want to do from a young age, and moreover, have the talent to take them far in that profession. Knowing your passion and being able to follow it goes a long way toward making clear goals for yourself and maintaining a determined spirit to reach those goals.

The rest of us have to struggle and muck around a bit more. Either you don't know what you want to do right out of high school or college, or you find that what you thought you wanted to do actually isn't that great, or you discover many unexpected hurdles and limitations to your choice.

The good news is that in the present day and age, you are not tied to one job in a single organization for your entire life. People can and do switch between multiple industries during their careers, wearing many different hats in the process.

Regardless of what you choose to do, it is the way that you do it, with a competitive drive and dedication, that will help you to succeed. There are few perfect opportunities, and success doesn't come overnight. It is the constant ability to seize the smaller, more common opportunities that yield success. Something has to power that competitive drive that keeps you motivated and prepared between successes. While the need to understand what drives you seems obvious, it does require time and self-reflection to figure out. Almost every adult gets caught up in the daily necessities of life and fails to step back regularly to think about the future. Don't let that happen. Take the time to ask yourself:

- What skills or activities do you like to do?
- Are those skills or activities found in certain professions, or are they hobbies you must pursue separately?

- How much does money factor into your decision about a career?
- How important is the balance of work time to personal / family time to you?
- What trade-offs are you willing to make in the above areas?

You don't have to tell the answers to these questions to anyone but yourself, but be honest with yourself on those answers. Doing so will go a long way toward picking the right profession.

What Do You Want to Do or Like to Do?

If you are one of the lucky ones who knows exactly what they want to do early on - building boats or being a veterinarian - your initial path is much clearer, though even then, vast differences exist between the various positions and specialties in a single profession.

If you have certain skills or pursuits you are naturally good at - such as art, cooking, or math - you have strengths you can leverage. Doing what you love to do makes you get up in the morning, full of energy, and go to sleep satisfied. Consider both "hard" skills - those that require specific technical knowledge or abilities - as well as "soft" skills - more intangible elements of how you think, communicate, and interact with others. Do you like meeting and working with people, or do you prefer to be alone? Do you think about the big picture, or do you prefer to focus on the details?

Take personality tests, talk to mentors and friends, read about different types of professions out there and figure out what appeals to you. Note what professions engage in the type of passions, pursuits, or skillsets that you enjoy. Spend the time doing this now to help inform your decisions. It isn't about picking a path that will dictate the rest of your life, but about getting into a habit of asking questions about where you are versus where you want to be.

Not many seventeen year olds have ever said, "I want to be an account executive for a plastics manufacturer when I'm older." Most people don't know what they want to do, and that's okay. If you aren't lucky enough to love a particular industry or hold a particular skillset, move on to the other questions on time and money. Two points of advice in that case: First, don't stop looking for the things that do combine personal passion and professional life, no matter how old you are or where you are. Second, don't sit around waiting for the answer to fall magically into your lap. Go to school, travel, or take an interim job until you find what you want to do. Standing still doesn't create progress. You may surprise yourself in the process, and in the midst of working in a job you didn't initially like, discover a new passion.

"Boring" Industries and Fields

At times, there are great perks in picking a position or job that most others don't find appealing. There is nothing wrong with big companies like Facebook or Google, or wanting to go into exciting industries like design or fashion.

Conversely, industries such as manufacturing or waste management attract many fewer people initially. Additionally, certain professional fields are often overlooked because they are thought to be boring, such as procurement or Human Resources (HR). A lot of potential exists in seemingly dull areas. Talented men and women who go into those industries and fields are often able to drive interesting innovations, as well as gain seniority more quickly than their peers who work in more competitive areas. Understand the trade-offs with these sorts of options. You might find that seemingly boring job has unexpected advantages.

Money

How important is the amount of money you make every year to you? Obviously, everyone wants enough to live comfortably, but that is still a very wide spectrum, based on personal preferences and the geography you live in. Ask yourself the hard questions such as: "Am I okay making $X right now, if that means I can afford maybe one small vacation every year, and have to watch my budget carefully?" You will have your own response here, and you need to be honest with yourself. For some people, making less while doing what they love is perfect. Others will say they are fine with the notion of doing something they mostly like - or even mostly dislike - for better pay and more financial freedom.

The top few percent in any industry or profession make a very comfortable living. With anything you end up doing - accountant or plumber, architect or pizza maker - being among the best in your peer group, and / or specializing in a particular sub-field, will achieve most, if not all, of your financial ambitions. Every profession can yield financial success.

To others with burning passions, money means nothing, as long as they can afford that passion and life's basic necessities. Where do you fall?

Personal Time vs. Professional Time

Perhaps you find that your personal passions don't connect well with professional options. In that case, you need to think about how not only money affects those options, but how free time does as well. Little to no free time to spend on things you love isn't a formula for happiness. There are 168 hours in a week; of that week, 40 hours is almost a fourth of your time spent working; 60 hours means over a third of your time. Let's say you sleep just 6 hours a day, that is another 42 hours gone by. In the rest of your waking hours, you have a little time for personal errands, sport, or leisure. How much of that personal time do you want or need?

Until you work a series of 60+ hour weeks, it can be hard to imagine what that sort of schedule does to your personal time. 60-hour weeks mean that you have either worked 8AM to 8PM for five of the seven days, or some of your weekend as well. Realistically if you want to be very good at your profession or make a lot of money, there will be crunch times that feature long work hours. Some career choices, such as consulting or being an entrepreneur, mean keeping that sort of schedule for long stretches. You can't know how you will feel about those kinds of hours until you experience them, but if you feel very strongly about, say, doing marathon training in your free time, or spending time with family, you will end up either having to pick one or the other, or letting both suffer. Become familiar with what a particular job or plan (e.g., starting your own company) entails.

At some point, no matter what the field, it will take not only skills and talent, but long hours. A lot of smart people want to get ahead, so you have to push that much harder than them. Momentum established early on can carry you far. You don't have to necessarily work long hours your entire career, but early on, when you have the energy and the time, it can be an opportunity to pull ahead of the pack. Are you willing to work those kinds of hours?

Think About You Constantly

What drives you one year to the next, or even one month to another will change. Devote some time to yourself regularly for reflection at least once a year; better yet, every three to six months. Ask yourself the questions from this chapter and think about what is good in your life, what is bad, and what has changed in your outlook. Life can speed by so quickly that we don't realize changes in our mindsets until we hit the pause button.

If you can discover what drives you, you will make opportunities happen for yourself consistently. The earlier you discover this drive and the ability to harness its energy, the more momentum you will build and the more potential you will unlock. In that spirit, the next chapter is for readers in high school and college who want to start realizing that potential as quickly as possible.

Chapter 2: For Those in High School & College

High School

If you are in high school or graduating from high school and reading this, you are already ahead in the game, because you are thinking about the future and how to prepare for its opportunities.

The thing about being an adult is that you have to live with the consequences of your decisions. But the best part about being young is that most of the bad decisions you make can be overcome and forgotten. Make as few bad decisions as possible that have a permanent impact on your future. Avoid the choices that make the path to success much more difficult.

The two big areas that almost always reduce your options for jobs and college are doing poorly all-around in school, or doing something illegal that stays on your record.

Fall in either of those buckets and you will need a compelling story to tell colleges or potential employers that you have matured or learned from your mistakes. Some options will be closed even then.

If you manage to avoid doing either of the above, few other decisions have such permanent impacts. You could be horrible in math but a wonderful writer, and you will be fine. School suffers somewhat because you are an amazing athlete, and you will be fine. Take a year off between high school and college to pursue a passion, travel, or save up money, and you will be fine. Life is a series of trade-offs; it is about knowing what those trade-offs are and their consequences.

The record book starts for almost everyone in high school. By your senior year, you already have three years of a track record that tells a story about the decisions you have made. Those decisions, together with your current plans, bring you to the one of the first major forks in life's path: whether to go to college (or a technical school) immediately, or instead work or pursue a passion. If you decide to go to college, choosing which college to go to will have a large impact on your options later.

While you are in school, live life to the fullest. That, of course, means spending time with friends. But also take the opportunity to explore passions and other pursuits. Use your weekends and summers doing interesting things such as interning for an organization or learning about the world through travel. While you will forget almost all of the parties from high school, you will remember the more special experiences.

By your senior year, it seems like you are on top of the world. You think you know everything. Senior year is also the time that the bigger decisions start to be made, such as college.

There are two good arguments for going to college. First, college or technical school is the place to learn more advanced skills that will be required by many jobs. Second, college gives you a chance to pursue passions and discover new things on a deeper level than high school. If you don't know what you want to do, you will have two to four years to discover many different fields, skills, and types of knowledge.

If you don't or can't go to college, it certainly doesn't mean your life is over or that your life will stink. Maybe the realities of life mean you have to work full-time right away. Maybe you pursue a passion such as a sport or you start your own company. Any and all of these paths still give you opportunity for success; many people never go to college and achieve great things. No matter what you are doing, if it is a type of work, you can still apply each and every concept written here.

For Those in College

In college or technical school, you start to focus on picking a profession and planning what your moves will be after college. You still have plenty of time to explore; take advantage of that time! College starts to combine the knowledge in the classroom with the world after school. If you major in English or creative writing, you are developing your own unique writing style. If you are an engineering major, you are studying the math and science that will allow you to build wonderful things.

Even if you think you know exactly what you want to do professionally, dive into different opportunities. Some professions post-college don't require a degree within that particular field. For instance, marketers don't all come from schools that offer marketing degrees; some marketers have degrees in psychology, some in economics or history. You may take a class or classes that change your mind or help you identify an even more specific area to focus on. You may take classes that spark lifelong hobbies or passions on a subject.

As for social life, enjoy it! On one hand, you can socialize at any age. On the other, socializing during college is a special experience. You learn new things, meet interesting people, and often make life-long friendships during college.

The decisions you make now are going to be more serious and should have more thought put into them. Yes, you can major in one area and work in another field. Yes, you can go to graduate school and change your profession later. But these decisions are in the scope of years of your life. You don't have to stress out about this; college is the place where you have the time to make those decisions. Spend some evenings deep in thought after you've experienced new things, and constantly think about what you want to do and what is important to you.

A good number of men and women start college ahead of peers because of college credits accumulated while still in high school. But only a few start their careers with professional knowledge and skills that separate them from other new graduates. Most just barely keep up as they learn during their first real job.

The secret is that you can learn and start applying many professional skills in college through mentors, internships, self-education, and student organizations.

Outside of classes and social life, you might start to engage in pursuits that influence and / or accelerate your professional career. There are an extraordinary amount of student organizations on most college campuses. You are going to be surrounded by a lot of people and ideas of all different types, and those experiences help you understand what you like and don't like. That might mean learning from or working in a student organization. Maybe you gain some knowledge, maybe experience, maybe leadership opportunities, maybe all three. Start-up businesses are easier to get off the ground than ever, courtesy of technology; perhaps you start a venture with some friends.

Then you have the summers, spent either traveling or working. You can try working for small organizations or large ones, in a number of different fields.

All of the above taken together can go a long way to shaping your ideas about what you want to do professionally after school ends.

Chapter 3: Finding & Evaluating Job Opportunities

If you are reading this chapter, you have hopefully picked an overall industry or field. If you haven't, don't stress. Your first choice doesn't commit you to doing the same thing for the rest of your life. If you aren't passionate about a particular area yet, choose the one that is the least offensive.

Heck, even if you still have no clue as to what you want to do, and right now you are scanning job postings, thinking of applying to anything that sounds like it pays half-way decently, it is never too late to start making more strategic decisions. Given that the job – whatever it may be – will occupy much of your life going forward, it pays (literally) to maximize your potential of finding great jobs, evaluating them, and getting them.

Even if it doesn't seem like you have the time, make the time to carefully evaluate options. There are a lot of jobs out there, and they are not all the same.

This is where careful research and planning separates the average or typical applicant from the great one.

Industries vs. Fields (Roles)

For those who don't have a particular industry in mind yet, begin your research by studying different types. Industries can start as broadly as education, aerospace, finance, and retail, and become as specific as kindergarten education, jet propulsion, insurance, or shoe retail. Roles begin as broadly as sales/marketing, operations, finance, or information technology (IT), and narrow down from there to specializations in paid search marketing, restaurant management, actuarial accounting, or computer repair.

If you know only the industry you want to go into, your next step will be to hone in on all of the jobs available to your experience and qualifications, and then categorize them by the major roles in the organization. Of the jobs you believe you are qualified for, what seems the most interesting? Different roles yield very different career paths.

If you know the role but not the industry, you can better gauge some core components such as advancement opportunities and average compensation, but even those can fluctuate wildly between different types of industries. A newly-minted accountant who starts working for a small business might make half the pay of an accountant who goes to work for a major accounting firm with bigger clients, or a tiny company that pays top rates for good talent.

If you have identified both the industry and the role you wish to pursue, your pool of potential jobs will be smaller, and your search more tightly focused. The wild card comes in deciding how far geographically you are willing or able to search for positions. Even in a big city, some niche job types only have openings a few times a year. Geography will greatly narrow or widen the scope of opportunities for you to consider.

Evaluating if You Should Apply for a Particular Job

Identify the perfect job for you. What does that role look like, and what are you willing to sacrifice? For instance, it may be a perfect job, all except for the fact that it requires you to move 300 miles away. Are you willing to do that?

Picking a job means picking an organization. You have to take your passions and your skills, and figure out what that translates to in possible career paths. As you begin to look at specific job postings, find out the following for each:

- Requirements for the job and / or the ability to learn those requirements through on-the-job training
- Compensation, both current and future potential
- Opportunity to learn and grow your skills and knowledge
- Opportunity to advance in responsibility / seniority in the organization
- Culture of the organization, including work-life balance and size of the organization
- Any other decisions, requirements, or sacrifices that must be made, such as relocation, to get and keep that job

Judge every opportunity by these key points. Comparing options side-by-side is a great way to look at multiple pieces of information at the same time. Create a simple table - paper or digital - with the above factors, as well as any of your own choosing, and be methodical with your evaluation. Take the time to think through the positives and negatives of each option.

The goal is to eliminate the positions that aren't as promising and focus further attention on the ones that are. Some of the key points, such as the opportunity to advance, aren't easily found out before you speak with someone at the organization, but you should glean enough information from the job postings themselves and research ahead of time to remove probable duds. To go into further detail:

Requirements for the job. Do you have the skills or background required in the job posting? If you don't have the necessary abilities but the job sounds amazing to you, you can plan a path to build the skills or experience to get there. Sometimes you may be just slightly short of the requirements, such as having two years of experience versus three. In those cases, if you feel you make up for it by depth of talent or other traits, still apply. Don't waste time and energy applying to positions that you would never be considered for. (This may sound obvious, but many job candidates apply to every ad with a shotgun approach, hoping something will stick, versus crafting a complete application package tailored to a specific position.)

Compensation. What is the average salary for a particular job? The job posting is the first source of information, but many job listings don't put exact salaries or even ranges. You do want to know the salary range before you apply, and especially before you begin speaking with anyone inside of the organization. The easiest and most accessible way today is to use website search engines to look up salaries by job title and industry. Then, if you do find a position that pays less than the average amount, you need to weigh that against the other (if any) positives.

Opportunity to learn and grow your skills and knowledge. Where is this position going to take you? Is it teaching you anything that will help you in your career later? You can figure it out by reading about a particular type of job, or better yet, speaking with someone who actually does that job for a living. Few people will ever turn you away when you tell them you are curious about what they do for a living and that you would like to learn more. The potential employer is a source as well. Is the expectation that you start working day one with a certain level of skillset that remains flat? If not, what resources are available for you to learn the job and skillset, including the employer paying for continuing education?

Opportunity to advance in responsibility / seniority in the organization. This ties somewhat into the above key point, but is the next step. Once you have the skills or experience from having been in that position, what are the possibilities to get a promotion, get a raise, or have more say in projects you take on and how they are structured? You might land what seems like a great job in a small company, only to find out that, a few years later, you are stuck in the same job while others have been able to advance into more senior roles elsewhere. Or the converse might be true; it may be a small company, so you ultimately jump from your current position to a much wider-spanning role or seniority level more rapidly. The key information source for this comes from the potential employer.

Culture of the organization. Culture stems from many things: the industry, the size of the organization, location, etc. It is the atmosphere at work and the colleagues that will make a job feel like torture or like a fun experience. With larger organizations, there are books and online guides that give you an insider's perspective on what it is like to work for that particular organization. The real flavor, however, comes from interaction with the organization. Not only interacting with your potential boss, but interacting with as many people as possible to get a sense of what that culture is like during interviews or onsite visits.

Any other decisions, requirements, or sacrifices that must be made. Almost every job at every organization has trade-offs. Figure out what those are. Will you have to relocate for the position? Are the hours odd or long? Do you have to travel regularly? (Work travel is not fun most of the time.)

At the end of the day, the above information allows you to filter down a range of possible jobs into a smaller group of positions you feel that you want to apply for. If at all possible, don't apply to positions you have no interest in, unless or until you have weighed the trade-offs, such as high pay or favorable hours.

Sometimes it is a financial necessity to find a position as

quickly as possible so that you can pay the bills. If you need to do that, do it, but don't then settle into a status quo. It is hard to both work a job (or for some, multiple jobs) and simultaneously spend the large amount of time it takes to conduct a job hunt. Those are defining moments though. If you want something bad enough, you will find the energy and drive to overcome obstacles and excuses.

Finding Job Opportunities

Where do you find job opportunities? Obviously, major job posting boards (online and off) or newspapers are a source. Don't limit yourself though; a comprehensive screening yields sources that many people don't come across. Organizations use many different tools and methods to post jobs. In order to find all of the possible great ones, it is a good idea to be thorough and search among the following:

- Major job posting boards
- Newspapers (and their websites)
- Niche job boards, especially online, for certain specialties
- Industry magazines and associations
- A company's website (especially larger ones)
- Referrals from your friends and professional network for job openings they know about and believe for which you fit the requirements (a massive source for actual hires)
- Your school career services department (many of them support alumnae as well)

Being proactive never hurts either. If you wish to work for a specific company, keep in touch with its managers and HR department for new openings. There is no harm in asking politely and professionally.

Don't get lazy in researching potential jobs. The more time you spend, the more opportunities you will find that best match what you may be looking for.

Section Two: Applying to Jobs

You have narrowed your job search down to positions that look promising and meet your criteria. Now you obviously want the job. Get it by standing out from all of the other applicants.

Most positions - especially the more common ones or entry-level ones - receive hundreds of applicants. That's a lot of people, all often competing for just a single spot. How do you stand out as the best applicant, the person for whom the organization says, "we must have that person for the position, they would make a stellar addition to the team."

The entire job application process is often described as a big funnel that begins with many applicants, and screens out a number with each successive stage. People apply to twenty jobs with an application and resume, hear back and interview with seven, and then get one or two job offers. Treating the process like a funnel is fine, but set aside thinking of it like a mass-production assembly line. Apply to fewer jobs, with more craft and care, and you will create a much more rewarding process.

The average applicant creates a resume that gets updated maybe once before he or she begins applying to jobs. Almost every job posting he or she applies to gets the same resume with a generic email of, "Hi, I'm great. Please consider me for the position." That is the norm.

Those who want to stand out and improve their odds follow a more detailed series of steps:

1) Keep a core resume up-to-date.
2) Learn about the organization, in detail.
3) Customize the resume and cover letter to each position.

4) Apply.

5) Repeat steps 2 through 4.

You can be successful in any position, but the goal is to find the paths that make it easier to attain that success. Choosing the right company, that has the right opportunities, is one of the largest shortcuts.

Chapter 4: The Resume

Especially if you are applying to a job "cold," meaning without a referral or introduction, your resume is the first essential item that decides whether or not you continue in the consideration process. Don't overlook the importance of this document, and be sure to spend the time to make it strong.

Review the guidelines below, consult numerous sources on resume creation, and most importantly, spend time revising your resume and having it looked over by others! You may think your resume is good (because you wrote it), but it might have some big holes or issues, or it might paint a picture of you that is different from the one you wish to convey. Don't underestimate the value of multiple perspectives.

Be prepared to discuss every element of your resume and explain it in more detail. Not only what you have included, but what you have not, such as holes in your employment history. Assume everything you have written will be challenged and / or verified.

Structure of a Great Resume

Long and windy, or short and powerful? Which type of resume do you think fares better? The short and powerful one. Keep your resume concise, mentioning your key achievements and accreditations. One to two pages is the maximum. The average resume reviewer spends under a minute glancing at a resume for initial consideration. Some companies now even automate the initial round of resume screening by hunting for keywords; if your resume doesn't contain those words, it never gets in front of a real person. Assuming you have a real person scrolling through your resume, you want to give them an immediate impression of, "Wow, this person seems like they could be a really valuable contributor."

Even men and women who are twenty or thirty years into their careers and have excellent achievements to show often curtail their resumes to a few pages. If they did something amazing fifteen years ago, they may document it in cases where that experience is relevant to the position they are applying for, but otherwise an employer will be more interested in recent accomplishments. (Note: there is something related, called a Curriculum Vitae (CV) which is a complete list of professional experience. Some technical fields may require a CV instead of a resume because time does not make a difference on the experience. In those fields, you should have both a resume and CV prepared.)

Here are the core sections of a resume:

1) Name & Contact Information
2) Experience
3) Education
4) Relevant Skills & Interests
5) References

Details on each of these sections follow:

Name & Contact Information

You can figure out name and contact information yourself. The one tip here: Don't use an odd personal email address, such as redwhitechili83@emaildomain.com. Stick with some variation of your first name and / or last name.

The Experience Section

Think you are incredible in a particular area and want to showcase how well you have done it historically? Great, but here is some context: Every resume starts that way. Words such as "excellent contributor," "outperformed," "thought leader," and "driven professional" are in almost every resume. They don't say, "extremely average worker, please hire me." Plenty of resumes convey mediocrity overall, but no one ever *says* they are average outright. You need to be specific and clear as to what your contributions were. The Experience Section is the heart of your resume. It is the place in which you want to show how valuable you have been to other organizations.

The best way for making yourself stand out is to frame your experience with the following structure. For each separate bullet point of each job you have previously held, use this formula: I did or managed X with tool or process Y that resulted in Z, where Z is a strong contribution, improvement, or superior result versus others in that role. (You can flip it to be: I achieved Z during X by doing Y). This framework specifically showcases what you have done, with the resources at your disposal, to affect real differences in the organization(s) you worked for. Very few resumes showcase results in this sort of concrete way. It will make you stand out. Examples:

EFG Restaurant
Shift Manager
- Trained 27 new servers over twelve months (X) with restaurant training regimen and my additional training guides (Y). 90% of these servers stayed with the restaurant longer than six months (vs. 65% average). My training regimen was recognized by senior management and adopted as standard. (Z).
- Increased 11am to 3pm gross sales by 17% (Z) during my shift (X) by creating a new special take-out meal for on-the-go moms and marketing to them (Y).

HIJ Services Company
Content Writer
- Wrote approximately 2000 pages of content (X) using *Manual of Statistics* (Y) compared to the 1600 pages goal. (Z)
- Created a new digital line of business for the company (Z) managing freelance writers (Y) by writing content for client website assets (X).

KLM Products Company
Sales Coordinator
- Responsible for sales in the California territory (X), I created a new sales presentation focused on client successes (Y) that led to outperforming my territory sales goals by 430% (Z).

- Given project of improving our sales database (X), I worked with the technical team to create new processes (Y) which led to a 30% reduction in training time and $150,000 in new business from better tracking of dormant-yet-still-viable leads (Z).

Be specific about how your contributions moved the needle for the organization. The value of that specificity can't be overstated.

Certain professions allow you to include examples or provide a link to a place where the resume reader can see for themselves a tangible example of your work or contribution. For example, if you work in a position where you create marketing campaigns or artwork, provide links to your portfolio. Like your resume, it should be carefully organized to provide examples relevant to that specific position.

For those applying to their first "full-time" job: Concerned that you don't have the type of experience described above? You most likely do. You have two major sources that you can draw upon to put in your resume. First, your part-time and summer jobs. What did you do there that was above average or showcases elements that will make you a great contributor? Second, clubs and extracurricular activities in college or even high school. Did you do something special or get a leadership position? If you are still using these achievements five years into your career you might have a problem, but otherwise you are expected to use these sorts of things as you don't have other experience to draw on yet.

Other than that, simply include the organization, your title(s), and the length of your employment / involvement. You typically start with the most recent and work your way down. You can opt to put the experience most relevant to the position you are applying for at the top, but the cover letter is another option to highlight relevant experience.

If you have received any awards or prizes that relate to the work you do, mention it in the Experience Section as well. Either at the bottom of the section, or below the job during which you received the prize. For example:

1st Place Winner
Tom Bradley Architecture Competition – August 2014

Education Section

You have a choice as to where to put the Education Section. Some people like to put it before (above) the Experience Section, while others put it after. Generally, the Education Section should be placed below the Experience Section for anyone who has been working for a few years. By that point, you should have some compelling accomplishments that you want to convey to the resume evaluator first before they read about your education. The exception is if you are still in school or fresh out of school, or your education is highly relevant to the position. Fair warning though, certain schools aren't always a positive. Some institutions have a reputation for churning out students in great numbers, while others have a reputation for graduating students that never seem to do well with a particular employer. Many employers could care less about the school you attended and focus entirely on the results achieved in your previous positions.

Regardless, you do have to list your education somewhere on the resume. It is pretty straightforward: School(s) attended, dates during which you attended them, and degree(s) obtained. Any postgraduate coursework should be included as well. If you took certain courses or tracks that are relevant to the position to which you are applying (for example, a position that requires some knowledge of accounting practices), break out that coursework as a bullet point underneath that particular school. One other tidbit: Once you have graduated college, don't put your high school on your resume.

Relevant Interests Section

This is the place to highlight some of your other strengths and points of interest. You may include:

- **Technical Skills**. Various knowledge and specializations in your particular field or industry. Don't put basic things like word processing or spreadsheets here unless you really are better than the average person in using them. Be specific about your aptitude in each technical skill listed.

- **Soft Skills.** These are skills related to communication and interpersonal relations. Languages are a big one and of special interest to many employers, though akin to technical skills, do not list fluency in a language unless you have real fluency. Don't put general statements like "strong manager" here. Present your management skills with specific examples in the Experience Section.

- **Relevant Personal Interests and Achievements**. This information will provide the most direct color on who you are as a person. What are the really interesting personal things you like to do that display traits like perseverance, or hard-work, or that you are great organizer? Put them here. Sports are often listed in this part as examples of these sorts of values. Be sure to list any leadership experience.

References Section

The majority of resumes don't contain a References Section, the most common answer being that a candidate doesn't want his or her references contacted by every job they apply to, only the jobs they are in late-stage contention for. That's a fair point. This the most "optional" section of all discussed here, but there is value in including it. A References Section showcases that you have people with whom you have worked who will vouch for you and your positive contributions in the past. They might be a peer, a supervisor, someone you have managed, or a mentor with whom you have never directly worked but serves as a character reference.

You should assume references will be asked for. Most employers ask for two or three. For example, anyone even just two years out of college, four references may be required. Some employers will require more references for more senior candidates. Have at least two senior / mentor references and two peer references. Add one reference for each additional one to two years of experience. If you are claiming to have managerial experience, have references from one or two people that you previously supervised.

As far as placing references in your resume, you can include the names and titles of your key references in your References Section, with the words "Contact Information Available Upon Request." This immediately shows the reader that you are ready and prepared without the worry about your references getting contacted too frequently.

Resume Styling

What is the visual look and feel of the resume? You have two major options:

- **Standard.** You stick to a safe font, your layout is primarily a single column from top to bottom, black text on a white background, and you don't include any designs or visual elements other than the text.
- **Artistic.** The font is something more creative / original (such as a cursive script), the layout might be different (such as four big boxes of information on a page), different colors for font and background, or visual designs starting with swirls and blocks and escalating from there.

For any non-creative / artistic position, stick with a Standard layout. Assume your reader wants to easily read about your achievements, not about your design style.

That said, you can still increase the polish on the Standard style. Bold the important places, have precise lines of separation between sections, and ensure that the formatting is standardized. One elegant addition becoming more common is the inclusion of a column on the left-side or right-side of the resume, which most often has the Education Section information inside of it. It breaks up content nicely.

For creative / artistic positions, you have a choice. With either Standard or Artistic-style resumes, you should be providing samples or links to samples of your work. If you do choose to showcase some of your creativity or design aesthetic via your resume design, go for it, but do get feedback from friends, colleagues, or mentors. Your resume may be visually stunning and separate you from other applicants, or it may be less beneficial than you think.

Look at other resumes, get feedback from others on your own, and really spend the time crafting something of quality. Don't forget to proof for simple errors.

To see a sample resume based on this entire section, check out http://www.succeedbig.com/sample-resume .

Lastly, ensure that you keep your resume updated. When you

work in a position for even six months, you are going to forget some of the details of the accomplishments you should be highlighting in that resume. Keep a running list that tracks your strongest moments or achievements. That way, when you do go to update your resume, you just need to pick the best of the best, drop those into the right format, and you are ready to go.

Your resume is a critical document. Spend the time to make it shine.

Chapter 5: Research & Customizing Your Application

You've got a strong resume. Great. The next step is to dedicate the time to research the position you are applying for. During interviews, many candidates ask basic questions about a company that they could have easily researched by visiting the website. There isn't anything horribly wrong with asking those types of questions, but on the other hand, you will impress your reviewer or interviewer much more by showing them that you have already learned everything publically available and now wish to dive into more sophisticated questions.

The good impression begins with the initial application. To make it special, spend the time to educate yourself on the organization. For something that is going to occupy a large amount of your life, you should want to learn everything possible about it.

Investigate:

- **History and background of the company.** How large or small is the organization? Does it have a good reputation or not? Is it a well-established organization or a young one? Does it seem to be growing and innovating?
- **The competition.** How does the organization stack up against competitors in what it does? Do its brand or results seem to be better or worse? Figure out if you are applying to the leader in the industry, or the middle or lower-tier. Learning about the competition also gives you insight that you can turn into good questions or observations later in the interview process.

- **The industry.** What does the broader industry look like? Is it growing or shrinking? Where are the opportunities to make a mark? Like the competition, learn what you can so you come across as an informed candidate for the position. It is common for people in a particular role or field to switch industries. You may know your former industry inside-and-out, but there are many nuances and differences between industries.

Where do you find this information? The internet makes things easy and provides three immediate sources: an organization's website, what other websites say about the company (review websites, salary-comparison websites, general informational websites), and financial sources (especially if a company is publicly traded on the stock market).

Tailor Your Resume

Once you have done your research, take a fresh look at your resume. Resumes are not very long documents, so you make trade-offs in what you can include. Sometimes it might be prudent to better highlight a particular accomplishment or experience that you believe a particular organization's hiring manager will be more impressed by. For instance, if you had experience in a prior job (or for younger applicants, in school) that applies very well to the position you are applying for, move that experience to the top of the section, or add in some more detail. When a hiring manager reads a resume that is not only strong overall but also seems highly relevant to the position, you get a real winner.

If you happen to be in a field where portfolios or work samples are common, similarly tweak them. Ensure you have selected the pieces that match up to the type of style and position. A good but non-tailored application doesn't stand out nearly as much as a tailored one.

The Cover Letter & Introduction

The cover letter is an underappreciated tool in the application process. "Cover letter" is a bit of an outdated term as most are submitted electronically these days, but what it really comes down to is a customized introduction that allows you to explain in more detail why you are the right person for the position. That introduction can range from a paragraph to a page. Don't go beyond that unless you are answering questions posed in the job posting.

The most important tip here: Do not include a "generic" cover letter or introduction that you send with every application. Any hiring manager with experience sniffs these out immediately and they make you look lazy. You can have a set of sentences that you re-use because they perfectly describe something you do or are good at, but otherwise customize the rest to each application.

The first type of content you can include highlights why you are a great fit for the position; relevant skills and experience, or a seeming alignment in beliefs or thinking. That's the common structure employed. The second type is rarer and revolves around including a deeper comment, observation, analysis or sample that really showcases your approach and tells the reviewer that you've spent time preparing your application. These observations or samples come from your research on the organization and industry. For instance, a salesperson might include some thoughts on how to build more business for the organization he or she is applying to.

Note that there is a small risk here with the second type of content; you may submit something that the hiring organization thinks is poor or inaccurate, removing you from further consideration. If you are afraid of that, don't include it, but if you are confident in your assessment or observations, it displays initiative. Keep the tone of the submission neutral. It is the submission that should stand out, not making yourself sound smart or superior.

Apply

Research done? Resume as good as you can get it? Created an application unique to the position? Time to apply.

Some organizations use software systems to collect applications. Here, fill out everything methodically, check twice for errors, and send away. Other job postings accept email submissions. In these cases, take the time to craft a good email subject line. Don't be overly fancy; keep it to the point and start with the core reason for the email. An example: "Job Application: Waiter with 10 year's high-end experience."

The cover letter often gets attached as a separate document to the resume. In cases where you have something that you believe is compelling or will set you apart from other applicants, consider creating just one document that first contains your cover letter, and then the resume on the subsequent page(s), to heighten the odds the cover letter is read before the resume.

When the cover letter comes in an attachment, you don't need a long introduction in the email body, but do use full sentences that clearly state you are applying for position XYZ and to please see the attached documents for reference.

Take one last look to review, and send your application off.

If you have been thorough in your research and your application, you have created a package that stands out from the competition and vaults you into the top tier of contention for a position.

The end goal isn't to maximize the number of positions to which you apply; it is to maximize the number of positions you hear back from for interviews.

Chapter 6: Acing the Interview Process

Arriving at the interview stage is a large step, as it gets you communicating directly with the organization - your potential future boss and other team members that you will be interacting with. You may initially deal only with a job recruiter or someone in the HR department. Be professional and accommodate all reasonable requests or questions.

Every organization structures the hiring process a bit differently. Some organizations that receive large volumes of candidates for similar positions simply set aside entire days for immediate in-person interviews. The most typical combination is a phone interview, followed by in-person interviews.

There may be an interim step between the application submission and actual interviews: Follow-up questions or tests. Organizations use these types of screening tools to further identify the top candidates. There isn't much detailed advice to provide on this point as every industry and every field will have different questions and tests. Just know your stuff. If you have done your research and applied to something you have the skill and experience for, you will be fine.

Once you get to the stage of actual interviews, you have two goals:

1) Sell yourself as the best candidate for the position
2) Obtain all of the information you need to make a balanced decision as to whether you want the position

It may seem apparent, but less experienced candidates often do poorly with that second goal.

Think like a Successful Candidate

Interviews produce anxiety in almost everyone, and it can be intimidating to speak with people you don't know who are assessing your possible worth. When you start to think like a top candidate (and you can do that even applying for your first job ever), you will have much more confidence. That comes with the ability to ask questions back. The application process should involve you evaluating the organization as much as the organization evaluating you. Get answers to all of the questions you have and be able to make an assessment of whether this opportunity is truly a great one for you; one that will help you succeed professionally in the short-term and / or the long-term.

Questions You Should Expect and Prepare For

There are a million questions a potential employer can ask. Here are the categories you should prepare for:

The achievements and experience included in your resume, cover letter, and / or introduction. Be ready to go into more detail on anything you have provided to a prospective employer. This information serves as the base from which a person begins to learn about you. How are the things you did special, or did everyone at your previous job accomplish the same thing? Some people overinflate their contributions (for instance, a colleague actually did most of the work). Questions also serve as way to evaluate your critical thinking and communication skills. The clarity (or lack of) with which you can describe what you are talking about is going to be a cue to an interviewer on how well you can describe a task or project to another team member or customer.

Each of your key skills. An interviewer wants to establish how basic or advanced those skills are. Anyone can put that they know how to use a program or perform excellent customer service. If you are going to be using those skills in the organization, the employer wants to have a fair gauge of them.

Job tenure and reasons for leaving. Organizations invest a lot of time and energy into hiring even a single person. They want to ensure that they are not speaking to someone with issues or tendencies that cause them to do their work poorly, or get along with others poorly, etc. If you have a history of positions with short tenures, you should have a good explanation, as that is often a red flag to employers. The most common - and accepted - reason for leaving a previous position is that it didn't have the opportunities you were looking for to continue your growth.

Tests of your logic and critical thinking. Organizations generally want to hire people who can think on their own. No smart manager wants to hire someone that requires constant supervision or guidance on even the most basic of tasks. Related to this, when a problem or crisis arises, will that person be able to come up with a response and act? Interviewers get at this by asking questions of your resume (above) as well as by giving you potential scenarios that might regularly occur in that position. You will either be leveraging your experience to come up with answers (you dealt with that kind of issue many times in a previous position) or you will have to produce an answer on the spot. The latter is a real indicator of how well you can think on your feet. Many organizations have trended away from what are called "brain teaser" questions such as, "estimate the number of jellybeans in a five pound jar," but depending on the industry to which you are applying, you might still receive them.

Discussion of your weaknesses. People hate these questions. You are trying to make yourself look as good as possible, and then you are asked about where you aren't so good. Think about it this way. No one is perfect. Even - and some would say especially - the men and women at the tops of their professions know they have weaknesses and come up with ways to minimize or remove them. The more you know yourself - the positives and negatives - the less the negatives impact you as you know how to deal with them. When a candidate struggles to answer these sorts of questions, they are typically overconfident, don't know themselves very well, or have something really negative they don't want to share. Spend time figuring out what you need to work on, and create the plan to do so; if it is a weakness that you just don't feel you can ever remove, think about ways to minimize its impact. Share the ways in which you have worked on those weaknesses or continue to work on them. It is that awareness of your weaknesses, and the improvement plan, which showcases your commitment to betterment and success.

What your goals and passions are. No employer wants to hire someone who just wants the job for the money or until they find something else. Expect questions on why you want the position, as well as what you envision yourself doing over the next couple of years.

Make sure to speak clearly and to the point in all of your answers. A vague response signals that you don't actually know what you are talking about. Think about your favorite topic in the world. You can speak for hours on it, right? Broad questions or detailed ones, you know the answers. Try to get to a similar level of fluency and familiarity on professional-related items; that will highlight your knowledge, dedication, and passion.

Ask Good Questions

Ask deep, informed questions. They show how you think through scenarios and make decisions. Good managers know that their team members are going to have many decision points each day to work through. Informed questions also make you seem more discerning about the opportunity, and less desperate to take the first position for which you receive an offer. That sets a strong tone.

The beginning of this section laid out ways by which to evaluate the opportunity a particular job might hold for your future. Much of that detail will come during the interview process when you speak directly to the interviewers. Here are some essential questions:

- What are the key goals of the team / organization?
- What will this position teach you?
- What is the promotion or growth track for the position?
- What about the organization's culture. What types of traits does the organization prize?
- Do you see any potential issues, or see any weaknesses (in skills, experience, approach) that give you pause?
- What sorts of tasks / projects would you be working on?
- What is the team (people you would be working with) like? Size, the way it is organized, how it functions.

(You should ask compensation questions. That part is coming up next.)

Come up with many more questions of your own that are suited to the position and industry you are applying for. For example, if you are applying for a marketing position, you may want to ask, "How has the company used social media to achieve its goals?" These types of questions showcase your understanding of the space.

You don't need to save questions until the end of an interview, though that will depend in part on the style and pacing of the interviewer. Some interviewers like to have more back-and-forth, while others prefer getting all of their questions answered first.

If you feel that you have held a real back-and-forth conversation with the interviewer by the time you finish, that is a great sign that you've made a connection and demonstrated your potential.

Practice makes perfect. Your first time doing anything is always going to be worse than your fifth time. Figure out answers to all of the main scenarios in an interview and rehearse them. Practice with your friends and mentors. That way, by the time you hit interviews, you will be much better prepared.

When You Don't Get a Job Offer

No one has a 100% success rate in applying to jobs. Other candidates might apply earlier and get the position before you get into final consideration, the employer might not think there is a fit, you might not think there is a fit, etc. Accept it, and most importantly, learn from it.

For any position for which you don't get an offer, thank the organization for their time and politely ask what exactly eliminated you from consideration, so that you can improve in the future. Some organizations won't reply or will send you a generic response later. Forget them. Others will provide valuable feedback.

Chapter 7: Compensation & Promotion Expectations

You likely know your own goals and targets for compensation and promotions, but do you know how to effectively ask for and structure these opportunities?

Once you have been working professionally for five or more years, you start to get a sense of *how* to ask for / optimize your financial earnings and your position in an organization. (Although some people don't know how to ask for these things twenty years into their careers.) It isn't something that is taught in high school or college, though many MBA programs do spend some time educating their students on the matter. Employers and organizations don't have much interest in educating employees on the subject either. Why would they, especially financially, when they get someone working for less than they could or should be paying? Not to say that all organizations are evil or that there are vast conspiracies everywhere. It is more that an organization creates certain financial goals and projections. The organization is accountable to its owners or shareholders, and it must at least break even (most years) to stay in existence. This holds true for non-profit organizations as well. A non-profit can't spend more funds than they take in year after year, or they will run out of money to pay for those commitments. (I do strongly believe in the concept of enlightened organizations that seek to make a "fair" profit that helps them support their employees as much as possible; there are numerous examples of such organizations.)

With most "average" organizations, there exists a lack of clarity in compensation and promotion expectations. Most mid-level managers don't have any of that sort of insight or control to boot. The truth is, most organizations fall somewhere in the middle of the spectrum, not actively working to better employee compensation, and not plotting a robot empire either.

The earlier in your career that you understand how to maximize your position, the better; not just the tips and tricks, but also about the perspective of an organization in the process. That organizational perspective is <u>not</u> about telling you, "organizations must lower costs, so live with the fact you will never make as much as you want to". The art of negotiating begins with understanding the other side's perspective, abilities, and limitations. That is how you know when to reasonably push for more compensation in an organization, and to know when pushing won't get you anywhere. The same goes for promotions.

An optimal structure looks like this:

- Do your research on standard compensation ranges for the industry or field to which you are applying, and how organizations structure compensation.
- Ask detailed questions of the potential employer on compensation and growth opportunities.
- Know what to ask for, when (and when not) to push back on a salary offer, and how.

Know the Numbers & How the Process Works

In the days of websites like Salary.com, it is amazing how many people don't know what the median compensation is for a position they are applying to. Median compensation changes according to the industry, the current size of the organization, number of years of experience, and the growth rate of that organization. Some small, high-growth organizations (also known as "start-ups"), supplement salary with stock grants and options. Large organizations do the same for senior positions. It "pays to know" how what you have been making in salary, or how much you want to make, compares against what other people are currently making. Keep track of this information.

Sometimes it actually isn't the potential employer that is underpaying, it is an applicant who made an outsized amount of money in a previous position; which is great for the applicant, but then that applicant needs to realize this and manage his or her expectations accordingly for other positions.

Some employers may be honestly paying less than the

industry standard because they are small, or they spend their dollars in other areas of the organization. If that is the case, you can decide if the other benefits of that particular organization outweigh a lower starting salary.

Good managers don't make decisions based on one candidate being slightly cheaper than another. Vast differences in salary is a different matter, but there is that old saying, "you get what you pay for." Good managers aren't going to worry about saving a few dollars as long as the applicant is within the budgeted salary range the position has been approved for. If that manager has $50,000, he or she is going to try and get the best possible candidate for $50,000, not a second-stringer for $45,000.

Most positions have hard-set salary caps, where they can't go above a certain approved threshold. Some managers have a bit of flexibility for a candidate who they feel very strongly about, around 5% or 10%. But if a manager goes, in turn, to their boss and says, "Well, I told you the position would cost us $50,000, but all of the great candidates want $65,000," they don't look like they know what they are doing. And if that is a constant theme, it looks doubly bad. In larger organizations, unless you are talking to a senior executive, they are not going to have a lot of latitude to change the numbers.

There are managers who will try to lowball you because they can. "Well, we were going to pay someone $50,000 for the job, but Sam came along and his range was $40,000 to $45,000, so we'll pay him $43,000." If you really think a potential employer is doing that, look to other opportunities, as there will be a pattern of this type of behavior.

Ask the Right Questions

A potential employer might go through some of the compensation information and growth opportunities with you, but they typically stick to what salary they can offer you and the fact that there are growth opportunities. Don't be satisfied by that; go further.

Compensation Questions:

- Besides the base pay, what is the structure of bonuses or performance awards?

- For sales / incentive-based positions, you should have many questions on the structure of those awards, as well as any limitations or caveats.
- How often are raises given and for what reasons?
- What other way(s) is performance rewarded financially?

For growth / promotion opportunities:

- To whom would you report?
- Is the position new, or are there others who are in it or who have done it?
- How often is performance evaluated and new responsibilities / roles given?
- Is there a specified average time in this position before you are eligible for promotion? Is it possible to get earlier promotions for excellent performance?
- In what ways is performance evaluated? What will you have to show the ability to do or manage to get a promotion?
- Is there a defined track to grow your abilities?

Note that you don't have to pose these questions of only your potential boss / supervisor. Much of the time you will speak with other people in the organization, and you can ask about the growth opportunities in a more casual way.

Know What to Ask for, When, & How

The first compensation-related element to surface (either on the application or via a question by an interviewer) is often a direct question on how much compensation you are seeking; either a single number or a range.

Unfortunately, many applicants, especially younger ones, when asked to write down salary expectations for a position or when asked during an interview, give a lowball answer. Sometimes it is because they actually don't know the salary range they should be asking for, other times it is because they think the person or organization hiring them will look more favorably upon them if they are "cheaper" than other applicants. Resist the urge to give a low number, no matter how much you want the job.

If you know what the average and top-end limits are for a

position, and you know what the minimum you are willing to take for a position is (including consideration of the other possible benefits of the job), your answer should be a precise one. The minimum you are willing to take is always your decision, but it shouldn't be much, if any, below the average or median.

- **If you are asked for an exact number**: Give your target number + 5% or 10% (as long as it stays within the top-range of positions such as yours).
- **If you are asked for a range**: Give a range between 90% and 100% of the top range. (As long as the 90% mark is equal to or greater than the average.) For example, if the average salary for a patent engineer with 2 years' experience is $50,000, and the top of the range is $62,000, you would provide a range of $56,000 ($62,000 x 90% = $55,800, then rounded to the nearest thousand) to $62,000 (the top of the range, 100%).

To do this well, you need to be honest in what your skills are and confident that you can sell the employer on those skills. If you do show them that you are a valuable potential asset, you will be in good stead. However, if you know you are lacking certain requirements or abilities, perhaps decide to be a little less aggressive. But it is almost better to apply to another type of position then.

An employer doesn't always have to be the first one to talk about compensation. In cases where the subject hasn't been brought up by the time you have arrived at the end an initial interview, you actually gain the advantage by being able to ask what the position pays. That reduces the chances of being surprised by a low figure later on, after you have invested even more time and energy in the hiring process, and you might even get a positive surprise on the amount. If you don't have any sense of what the position pays by the time you are doing in-person interviews, that is latest time by which to find out.

Now, what happens after you provide the number or range, or *you* ask the initial question? You will get a response. Sometimes immediately, sometimes later in the application process, sometimes all the way after interviews have been concluded and a formal offer is made.

Here are the possible outcomes:

- **If your desired number is agreed to:** Congrats, you got it. Don't worry about more upside you missed. Sure you might have gotten it, or you might not have because the employer already stretched to meet the number.
- **If you get a response better than expected:** Congrats.
- **If you have given a range and the offer comes back at the top or exceeds it:** Congrats.
- **If you have given a range and the offer comes back inside of that range but not at the top:** Counter. A solid counter is 3% to 5% of the offer made. If the offer was $50,000, counter with $51,500 or $52,500. Now you can be precise with figures. It is your discretion to counter higher.
- **If the offer comes in less than your desired number or range:** Here, too, is where you should counter. Counter in the same way as the previous scenario if still above the minimum you are willing to take.
- **If the number comes in below the minimum you are willing to take and you can't get the employer to raise it:** Move on. It is difficult, but if you have set an honest minimum, don't compromise.

The major factors that impact the ability for an employer to modify the offer are:

1) The amount of money they have budgeted.
2) Their ability or desire to go to their own boss (if applicable) to get more.
3) The financial condition of the organization. The organization may be having a tight period with profits or returns, the overall industry might be experiencing economic issues, or the entire economy might be performing badly, all putting financial pressure on the organization and limiting the ability to pay more.

Numbers 1 & 2 are the ones that allow for counter-offers and increases, as they relate to how much value the employer places on the position or how valuable they feel you might be to the organization.

Compensation negotiation can become more complex when you also throw in additional forms of compensation such as annual bonuses, sales and performance incentives, profit-sharing, stock grants, or stock options. This introduces a number of new dynamics, but the negotiation process remains the same. Do your research to be confident in what you should be asking for, and then you can get more creative. For instance, the offer may not budge on salary, but you successfully counter with receiving some additional stock options.

Conclusion

Great application. Strong interview. Well-negotiated compensation. Win. Win. Win. Do all of these things and you greatly increase your chances of success.

Once you get an offer, your references may or will be contacted and all of the other processes, such as background checks, will occur.

In any interim period before starting your position, wrap up other professional loose ends, and take some time to re-charge or charge up. The first weeks and months in a new job will be hectic. If you have time and want to get ahead, keep learning about the organization or industry where possible, or upgrade any skills that you think will be valuable to you; whatever you can do to hit the ground running on day one of your new job. Congrats.

Section Three: Maximizing Opportunities - Your Approach

You have a job. Maybe you think it is an amazing job, maybe you think it is average and just a way to pay the bills. If you love your job, it is easier to put in the energy to excel at it. If you don't love it, you need to channel energy from another source to put toward the job. The job may help you achieve other goals, or it may be a stepping stone to another position. Whatever your own case may be, find the energy.

There are some nearly universally-applicable approaches to being successful in a career. Put them to use in any type of job and you will accelerate your journey. Being successful in a role means contributing; not just as expected, but *more* than expected, *before* it is expected.

Chapter 8: Learn the Company. Own the Company

To be a strong contributor and enact real change, you must become very familiar with your organization. How can you execute at your full potential or contribute in the best way possible without knowing the organization and its industry? That sounds like a pretty broad statement, because it is a broad statement. Regardless of whether you are a clinician, a designer, or a retailer in a store, get an understanding of how the business works.

It is surprising (or saddening) when even people who have been at their jobs for over a year know little about how the business operates outside of their job function. This is unfortunately common. The good news for you is that, if you take the initiative to learn these things, you are placing yourself well ahead of most of your peers. Think of it this way: How much about the business do you think your boss' boss knows? Sure, if you spend five years somewhere, knowledge will naturally seep in, bit by bit. Instead though, approach this proactively and learn about the organization. It automatically puts you on the level of senior managers. Another common statement: "Well, I don't know what (Bob) does at the company." Unless Bob works in a top-secret area, Bob not telling you isn't the problem. You not asking is the problem.

Broad-based understandings of business principles, such as finance and strategy, are a key reason many people decide to pursue an MBA. But why wait until then to learn those things? You simply feed into many organizations' beliefs that a particular position requires an MBA. Be the person that breaks the mold and shows a skillset that neutralizes that requirement and vaults you into a higher level of responsibility.

How to Learn About the Company

Approach your knowledge gaps from the bottom-up as well as top-down. "Bottom-up" means from those people around you day-to-day and information available to you as an insider. "Top-down" is the broader organizational strategy and overall industry.

The bottom-up approach:

Ask your boss. Ask him or her about the organization's strategy. Any half-decent manager will be thrilled that one of their team would ask about the bigger picture. Most of the time, managers simply don't think about sharing the details as they are busy themselves, or they take it for granted that you know certain things. Do you understand what the goals of the company are? What function every person on the team performs to help reach those goals? What about the broader organization? What can you learn about the direction and the key initiatives that the organization is undertaking to reach its goals? What kinds of initiatives have been tried before that have failed? Your boss, especially if he or she is a senior manager, should know a lot.

Peer knowledge. The people who you work with are a great source of information. The more you know about their role on the team and in the organization, the better. They are working to achieve certain goals for the team, find out what those are. When you have lunch with someone, take the opportunity to engage with them; what they do day-to-day, how they do it, and why.

Sit-in on key internal and external meetings and events. Take every opportunity you can get to listen to conversations between your team, other teams, and between the organization and customers, donors, or vendors. As long as you are meeting your own assigned deadlines and tasks, and the conversations are not confidential, no one will mind you sitting in. There are far fewer "secret meetings" than most people think.

Take advantage of all of the material at your disposal. Start with the organization's website. Many men and women don't go through the entire website, aside from the career or staff sections when applying for a position. Most websites are a rich source of information and, more importantly, present the organization in the way that its executives or owners wish to position it. The organization's newsletter doesn't contain its inner secrets, but it will teach you about how the organization speaks about itself and important events. More than the newsletter, the typical employee has access to many internal files in his or her team, or even from other teams. When in doubt, simply ask to read or view something. Every part of an organization produces higher-level documentation on what they do.

The top-down approach:

Start at the industry-level and work your way down from there.

Industry Trends & Drivers. What are the things that make for a good year or bad in your industry? For instance, if you work in the oil services industry, cheaper crude oil prices might be good, or they might be horrible, depending on your organization's role. If your organization relies on high oil prices and they take a sustained dip, that will affect the growth plans of the organization (either pausing initiatives or forcing the organization to become smaller). If you work for a fast-food chain, are rising beef prices creating an impact on margins that, in turn, can make it harder for the organization to expand? If you work for a non-profit, certain types of news might be the main triggers for rises in donations. Understand the major forces that help to shape the direction of the organization.

Organization Niche & Strategy. Especially if you work for a larger or public company that issues annual reports on performance and goals, you have a wealth of information at your disposal. The vast majority of people in a public company have little idea of what is going on. Maybe they pay attention to the stock price, but they never read the real detail available in quarterly and annual reports. Your boss will certainly make clear what is important to their goals day-to-day, and month-to-month, but how do those fit into the larger expectations for the company?

The Competition. Every organization has competitors. Study what they do, how they do it, and their strategies compared to your organization's strategies. Does your organization seem to be doing better or worse than its competition? Which competitors are doing better, and why? Read their material, look at their marketing and sales initiatives, anything you can get your hands on.

The Customers. Something puts money into your organization's bank account. Non-profits have donors (and sometimes customers as well), most other types of organizations have what they call customers or clients. Do you understand who those customers are and what compels them to choose your organization?

It doesn't matter what position you hold; every position benefits from this type of study. All of this leads to a level of thinking and awareness far beyond the average person. It leads you to think like the owner of an organization.

The Ownership Principle

Pretty simple yet powerful notion: Make decisions as if you own the business or had founded the organization. All business owners or entrepreneurs understand this concept deeply. You look at your actions and decisions differently when you view yourself as owning something. A person's financial livelihood depends on an organization continuing to exist and doing well enough to employ them. Most people don't earn a living from an organization while simultaneously wishing it went out of business. But viewing an organization as your paycheck source, versus viewing the organization as if you owned it, are two very different things. The person concerned simply with their own position and compensation generally has an attitude of what you could call "casual indifference" to developments that don't directly affect them or that they don't *think* affect them.

This principle is not limited to entry or mid-level positions in an organization. Regularly, reports break about some CEO with a multimillion-dollar salary who seems completely out of touch with his or her customers and employees, operating out of self-interest versus the good of the organization.

On financial and budgeting decisions, men and women will spend money differently when they tie themselves more closely to the end result. Even a marketer, accustomed to spending large amounts of money on an organization's marketing, will often think differently about making dollar allocations as an owner of an organization company. He or she won't simply be content with only making his or her target goal, but instead will try to get every possible ounce of upside.

The ownership principle is not about always trying to save every last penny. Telling employees that they must use less than a certain amount of paper clips every year might save an organization money, but when you have people that begin to worry all the time about things not related to their key functions, those people often lose sight of larger strategic initiatives.

By the way, the example of paperclip tracking is a real example. A large company brought in "efficiency consultants" into a research and development (R&D) department. The very people who were supposed to be the most creative and focused on coming out with new product lines for that company instead had to begin worrying about their use of office supplies.

Take the above example versus a principle and philosophy of "I own the business." When you have that ownership value ingrained in an organizational culture, the vast majority of people are going to use only the office supplies they need. You can structure it a dozen different ways to keep a close eye on budget, yet not make everyone dwell on paperclips; have them thinking about why the organization keeps a close eye on the budget and how all of these things roll up together to keep the organization on firm footing. When this sort of ownership principle co-exists with collaboration across different teams and departments, the right sort of mindset emerges and magical things begin to happen.

Pride in ownership is an extremely strong concept. It stretches much further than directly financially-oriented decision making. The designer making a brochure for her organization will work that much harder to ensure the brochure is perfect. The retail associate will spend that much more attention on a customer and on noting possible improvements in the day-to-day tasks.

Where you really win by adopting the mindset is that most people in an organization don't take an ownership approach. The smartest organizations out there promote this principle as core value, but not even there do all people embrace it. In an average organization, you will join a small sliver of people who think in this way. That sliver of people are typically the senior managers who are heavily invested in an organization (financially and psychologically).

When you come into an organization as a twenty-something year old and think like a more senior employee with the ownership principle, your thinking will align with theirs. When these senior people see that you hold the same values, that you think not only about your day-to-day responsibilities, but also how your and your team's actions impact the broader whole, you will be recognized and tapped for further responsibilities.

If you feel as if your direct supervisor doesn't embrace these values, but the next level above him or her does, don't worry, all is not lost. Do not try to undercut your boss, but use opportunities you get (or make) with more senior managers to display your own thoughts and the actions you have taken. Make sure your actions reflect your ownership principle thinking and the results of those actions will filter up. You might be surprised how important casual conversations are to establishing credentials and career paths. The five minutes your boss spends talking with his boss about you, or the five minutes that you speak with your boss' boss one random day establish the impressions about how you think and what you value. Think like an owner, and prove that you execute very well not only on what you are given, but that you have an awareness of and interest in the overall organization. This mindset will take you far.

Chapter 9: Key Outlooks & Approaches

In addition to the ownership principle, there are a number of other approaches that will further the success you achieve in a position. This chapter contains the following topics:

- Do It Better
- The "How Can I Help You?" Mantra to Affect Change
- Question the Status Quo
- Failing Constantly to Improve
- What to Do When You Make Mistakes
- Building Improvements to Scale
- Anticipation

Do It Better

No matter how small or large the task assigned to you in a job, figure out how to do it better. Better can mean a number of things:

- Faster
- Cheaper
- Higher quality
- Increased results

Don't think simply about the task, but the process to accomplish the task. For example, a waitress might consider how to improve the happiness of her diners. She might work through different ways of presenting the menu to increase purchases of desserts. Maybe the waitress notices the bread always arrives cold to the table and works with the kitchen to time it better, so that it arrives warm. The waitress sees that the bathrooms get really dirty around 8pm, so she discusses a plan with the manager to increase the schedule of bathroom cleanings. And so on.

It comes down to the approach. Part of that approach is having the energy to dedicate yourself to the job. That, in turn, drives an awareness. It may take you some training to become more aware. A lot of people likely saw the issues the waitress in the above example had seen, but how many simply dismissed it instead of doing something about it?

With everything you do, ask yourself:

- What is the current way this is done?
- How can I improve it?
- Can I do more than I was asked to?

You'll notice too that the above example also includes observations that aren't directly the responsibility of the waitress, but they are the responsibility of the restaurant (organization). How many other waiters and waitresses do you think are being so proactive? Very few. Improve not only the things assigned to you, but work to improve those that aren't. In turn you will be noticed and stand-out from co-workers who work on simply the assignments given to them, with no further thought or ambition.

With any task that you are given, run through its various components and question the existing way it is done. This is very different from just getting a task and doing it like you have been told. It applies to every type of work in the world. If you are a receptionist, how can you improve the way the phones are picked up and enhance caller satisfaction? If you are an occupational therapist, is there a more effective or quicker way to process your patient's information? If you are stocking shelves, how do you do it faster and in ways that improve a customer's experience? You get the idea. To break it all down:

- Learn the way it has been done before by others. The tips and hints, the problems they've encountered that no one first told them about, etc.
- Question the historical ways of doing it.
- Create improvements in the process or task from your own experience or thoughts.

- Test those improvements.
- Get feedback from others.
- Keep the improvement cycle going.

Habitually work to improve upon the historical standard, and you will become the one who sets that standard. That is what leaders in an organization do.

The "How Can I Help You?" Mantra to Affect Change

There is a fine line between confidence and overconfidence (also known as cockiness). Sometimes we don't want to listen. Other times, we just think we know better, so we don't listen, especially when we are young.

Confidence isn't a bad quality; neither is ignoring the status quo. That's how you innovate. Learn to balance that though with a willingness to listen, to learn, and to make decisions after you have all of the facts.

The approach by which you seek to do your job and contribute more broadly is what matters. If you take an "I'm smarter than you" attitude, you are hurting yourself, as you turn even a simple exchange with another person from a logical discussion to one based on ego.

Adopt an attitude of, "How can I help you?". As an actual question you ask, and as a mantra that you hold yourself to. A mantra is a statement that is repeated frequently. Keep it in your head, and actually pose the question regularly to those with whom you work.

If you take the time to first be patient and listen fully to someone, and then ask, "How can I help you?", you align yourself with them. The amazing "trick" to this is that it actually makes even the hardest conversations easier. Especially as a young member of a team or organization, you don't want to create a "You vs. Them" dynamic with others who have been in the workforce for twenty or thirty years. A balanced, more mature approach is what convinces people to believe in you and to be open to your viewpoints.

Whether it be someone within your organization, a customer, or vendor, ask yourself first, "How can I help them?" Then ask them, "How can I help you?" Actually ask the question. Then listen closely. The response you get will be invaluable in framing your approach.

For example, let's say you are a social media manager, tasked with rolling social media out across an organization that has previously never levered it. You think you know everything about social media marketing (and maybe you do). When you introduce yourself, you say something along the lines of: "Hi, I'm the new social media manager. I have all of these amazing plans to make the company better with what I do. Listen to me tell you how I can improve your life with my magical tools." Now that example is a bit of an exaggeration, but many times that is how people come across.

Here's the better way to proceed: "Hi, I'm the new social media manager. My role is to support you in figuring out ways to use social media to grow the organization's brand. How can I help you do that?" If the responder has some thoughts, wonderful. You listen and appreciate the good ones and gently counter the not-so-good ones with your thoughts. If they don't have any, you can offer your suggestions. Not aggressively or by making them look stupid, but with a balanced proposal that focuses on improvements and benefits.

Don't underestimate the value of the "How Can I Help You?" mantra to get ahead. Not only does it help you get results for your work, it also identifies you as a team player that can effectively work with others.

Question the Status Quo

Innovation cannot exist without failure. It is the fear of failure - its costs financially, personally, and professionally - that keeps innovation from happening. When you stop learning and being open to change, you will stop progressing and stop innovating.

To keep failure in the right context and keep yourself thinking about forward momentum, adopt a practice of constantly challenging the status quo.

This concept appears after the "How Can I Help You?" mantra for a reason; questioning the status quo can be done tactfully instead of aggressively. Questioning the status quo by definition means you are challenging someone's practices and ways of thinking. Approach it the wrong way and you simply make people defensive.

Challenging the status quo circles back to doing everything better. Day to day, approach everything you do with an attitude of curiosity and fearlessness.

Failing Constantly to Improve

There are many management books and business biographies that discuss all of the "successful principles" that one particular person or organization has taken to establish their riches or legacies. Fewer books discuss failures in detail. Now, part of this is that most people don't chronicle or remember their failures as well as their successes, but the failures often teach you more. It is wonderful that a business book tells you the ten principles that are going to make you or your company a rock-star, but how were those lessons learned?

An example: you see [insert your favorite company brand here] constantly produce captivating marketing campaigns and taglines that increase their sales and awareness. Do you really think that company created just one marketing message that was perfect out of the gate? No way. That company – its people - worked through dozens, if not hundreds, of potential approaches. Many never made it out of the drawing room. Some number of potential ideas were trailed on small scales with test groups or isolated customer pockets. A select few finally emerged as winners. But the winners likely wouldn't exist without all of the losers before them.

A team that launches a product three months after the promised due date isn't getting a dozen roses. The entrepreneur who misses growth expectations by 50% isn't having a celebratory dinner with his or her investors. Big failures mean big consequences, we all know that. A swift exit from the organization and a tarnished reputation often result. Not only do we know it, but the fear of big negative consequences makes people afraid to take risks and drive change. Yet, without embarking on new initiatives, the organization won't grow or prosper. At best, it will keep pace with competitors; at worst, it will fall behind or wink out of existence.

There is another way to innovate much more quickly, safely, and with smaller consequences. That is to fail very often, on as small a scale as possible. Some examples:

- As a marketer, you can write dozens of iterations of ad copy, doing small tests with each one before committing larger dollar amounts into the best version.

- As a designer, you can make many designs that you evaluate with yourself or through trusted peers before showing it to a boss.
- A salesperson can construct half a dozen different sales pitches to test with prospective clients, to find which messaging works best.
- A chef can test new recipes with a smaller group of patrons before committing to putting it on the main menu.
- You have a presentation to make in front of a senior group of people. Draft that presentation and share it with others before the official date. Each version will get better and better.

Every job out there allows you to create an environment where you fail by yourself or within a small group.

Failing constantly and quickly allows you to discard what doesn't work that much faster. You are forcing yourself to be creative to come up with new possibilities to test. You learn from the wins and losses of those tests, you implement the improvements, and you start testing again. When you structure those tests properly, any incremental amount of time or money with little or no return is a drop in the bucket compared with chaining each small success to a subsequent small success. These small successes add up quickly.

Even for larger projects or initiatives that you are assigned, the same principle applies. If you set yourself up to be judged for big events a couple of times a year (or less), it only takes one negative result to make your overall results seem poor. Think about it like school grading. 3 out of 4 answers right, or 75%, is equivalent to a "C" grade in most school systems. You may not change the due date for the overall project in favor of many smaller ones *officially*, but you can break the project down into many smaller segments. Test and improve each segment, one after another, and soon you have an end product multiples better than the original.

Once you embrace failure as a positive consequence of creating upward momentum, you will never look at failure as a negative again. You will want to fail constantly in controlled ways to propel improvements over time.

What to Do When You Make Mistakes

You will make mistakes that are not small or planned. It happens. No one is perfect. What matters more is what you do after the mistake. The secret is speed: speed in communicating the mistake and owning up to it and speed in fixing the mistake. When you are talking about small or even medium-sized mistakes, the best approach is to quickly tell any parties whom it is affecting and to manage their expectations that you are working on fixing it (if it hasn't been fixed already). People don't like being surprised and they don't like being boxed in by being told of a problem last-minute.

For instance, an employee tells her boss: "John, that sales proposal was missing a key section when I sent it to the client an hour ago. I'm really sorry. I'm already working to correct the proposal and will have it to the client shortly."

Communicate it as soon as possible, don't sit on it. Mistakes typically only compound when the window to fix them comes and goes because you haven't owned up to the mistake and gotten others to help you fix it. In the example above, John the manager has a number of options to fix the issue when he learns about it. He can opt to either sit on the proposal until the new version is done or immediately contact the client to inform him or her of the issue. He can leave the employee to finish the proposal, give it to another team member, or decide to finish it himself. John has multiple options for how to handle the situation because he has been immediately informed. He is also less likely to be angry learning about the mistake now, versus the next day or when the client brings it to his attention instead of having heard about it ahead of time.

Deal swiftly and openly with mistakes. Enough said.

Building Improvements to Scale

Clay receives an assignment from his boss to conduct a training later in the week on a topic that he knows well. Clay's boss has historically done this training, but it isn't a large amount of responsibility and it is felt that Clay can get it done. (It can be any topic: a software system, a therapy regimen if you are clinician, a machine process, how to paint molding...anything.) Clay scribbles down a few notes in his free time and ends up spending four hours doing the training. He does a pretty good job and everyone is satisfied. A month later, Clay has to do the same training. He digs up his notes and proceeds to do the training in about the same time, four hours. Clay does the second one a little better as he is now more comfortable with the role, but really it ends up being the same training his boss has done for multiple years. No better, no worse.

Clay didn't do anything horribly wrong, but he did miss two valuable opportunities:

- The opportunity to improve the process and / or improve the results.
- The opportunity to systemize the process or task for the next time it is required.

Beyond simply improving what you are given, go a step further and "systemize" it. Create a process that can be used or duplicated by others. If you are given the responsibility for compiling a monthly report, build a template or format that cuts down the time and work required to assemble it. In the example with Clay above, Clay could have created a written document or recorded the training. If he realized that the training takes place about once a month and he always gets a certain set of follow-up questions, Clay could have been proactive and set up monthly primary training sessions with a shorter follow-up ten days later. Suddenly, Clay has created a system for training for which he will ultimately receive credit as his superiors see the benefits therein.

Everything that you do, if there is even a chance that you or someone else will have to do it again, create a system or process for the next occurrence. That can be a set of directions, a template, trainings, some tools to save time, etc.

You will not only exceed the standards and benchmarks expected of you, but also create a reputation as the person to go to because of your insight and dependability. That's a good reputation to have.

Anticipation

Anticipation is the way you wow your supervisors, peers, and customers. Anticipation is the skill of thinking ahead to what another person is going to say or ask for, before they actually do. Take this common situation:

Boss (asking the same question every week): Jake, could you pull the sales numbers for the week?

Jake: Sure boss, I'll have it for you in a few hours.

Jake's response isn't horrible, but his boss would be a lot more impressed if it went like this:

Boss: Jake, could you pull the sales numbers for the week?

Jake: Already did it, boss. They were 10% better than we expected, because Customer X decided to open a new location...

This time Jake not only anticipated a request he should have known was coming, but performed a logical next step in wondering "why is my boss asking for it?"

Some of you are reading this and saying, "duh, obviously" or you might be thinking Jake's boss could have just told Jake, "have the numbers for me every Friday morning, with your analysis attached." You would be right that Jake's boss should be doing that for any regular need or task. Each week though, there are dozens of situations that come up, some repetitive, some unique.

If Jake's boss is making a conscious effort to develop Jake's logic and problem-solving skills to set him up for more responsibilities, he is going to measure how often Jake waits for him to say something, versus how often Jake proactively completes tasks and comes up with ideas without being asked. Should Jake's boss not purposefully be giving Jake such tests, he is still going to form a positive impression about Jake's proactive attitude. Jake wants his boss to feel "I'm glad Jake got X or thought of Y for me, I can always depend on Jake".

With co-workers, the concept remains the same. When Jake uses a proactive approach and anticipates the needs of his co-workers, they will appreciate the forethought. With customers or vendors, the same methodology applies. To build a habit of anticipation:

1) Study where repetition occurs.
2) Put yourself in the shoes of your boss, team member, or customer.
3) Plan where and how you can take the action before you are asked to do so.
4) Execute.

Repetition also extends to questions. For example, a certain type of customer routinely asks the same types of questions when you interact with them. Internalize that and proactively incorporate the answers to those questions with the next customer of that type.

This all has the added benefit of you and your boss, team, or customer spending less time communicating about the basics and more time on sophisticated discussions around tactics, strategies, and new initiatives.

Chapter 10: Tactical Thinking

To make far-reaching contributions, it is important to develop your tactical abilities.

Strategy is the creation of the plans that guide you, your team, or the organization to achieve its goals. Part Two of the book goes into greater depth on strategy development. Read those sections even if you are not a manager or not actively creating strategies yourself. Become aware of how they are formed and contribute to them where possible.

Tactics are the "how are we going to do this", the day-to-day and week-to-week tools, methods, and approaches that fulfill the strategy. At any level in an organization, you are part of the tactics, a resource to the larger whole. While you may not be a manager involved in strategy development, you can always step forward to drive tactical initiatives. To do so:

- Absorb the goals of the organization and team.
- Figure out the strategies in place to attain those goals.
- Study the current tactics in place to get there.
- Identify your role in executing those tactics.
- Expand and innovate upon those tactics to increase performance.

A previous chapter covered the concept of truly understanding your organization and its strategies. You should also know your own current role (obviously), but then you need to understand how your role fits into and contributes to the tactical plan.

Example: A pet store wants to increase sales by 200%. That's an organizational goal. The strategy it develops to achieve that goal is to create a new, robust website that allows it to sell its products online; its current website only lists its location and hours. The strategy breaks down as follows:

1) Create the website platform.
2) Upload all items for sale to the website.
3) Change operational processes to allow for digital orders.
4) Market the website to drive customers.
5) Maintain the website platform.
6) Fulfill orders coming through the website.

Tactics are the requirements that go into each of the above pieces. The way to get the website built and maintained, the creation of methods to facilitate product order flows, all of the daily operational actions that must be done well for the strategy to come together.

Assess how much of your time is being spent accomplishing tasks that directly relate to the primary strategies of your organization. Do you ultimately spend 10%, 30%, or 90% of your time helping achieve the key strategies? Or do you spend more time on non-key tasks and activities? You can innovate and excel at either, but you will gain more recognition and standing for aiding the team or organization on its primary strategies.

To extend the above example, the pet store has a team of three customer service people that answer phone calls and emails from customers that have an issue. You are one of those three people. As soon as you are made aware of the organization's strategies, you can step up. Be proactive and come up with a customer service plan for the new orders and related issues that will come from the website. You can volunteer to help upload items or proof the website for errors. You can learn additional skills that allow you to do basic maintenance on the website. Suddenly, you can go from having little impact and involvement in critical areas to being a central player in a new strategy.

Take on New Responsibilities

A hallmark of succeeding big professionally is to not only do the tasks assigned to you well, but to seek opportunities beyond them to contribute.

When you have an understanding of the things that are most

important to an organization, you know which responsibilities to volunteer for that can or will make the most difference. You can:

- Develop new skills that allow you to participate or take the lead in critical areas.
- Extend responsibilities to parallel areas in the organization that operate worse than your area.
- Extend responsibilities that utilize your skills in new, but related ways.
- Teach your skills and share your tactical thinking with others.

Every type of position out there crosses over in some way with others in the organization. A print materials designer might volunteer to apply their skills to a website design or designs for job posting advertisements. A person in the finance department can work with almost any department to help them craft budgets or reduce expenses. The most efficient welder in the organization can show other welders his or her skills.

Understand your role and where you can pivot and extend.

Innovate on Current Practices

Constant attention to improvement and a willingness to test new things are core ways to innovate. But how do you think up ways to innovate? It can initially sound easy to say, "plan up a dozen different ad campaigns and test them", instead of just one or two. But where do you find the inspiration and ideas for all of those new variants?

Think of innovation at both the micro level and macro level, originating both inside of the organization as well as outside of it.

Companies that fail to innovate, fall behind. They either go out of business quickly as competitors leapfrog them with new technologies and solutions or they suffer a slow death of a thousand cuts. "Slow" is a relative term, but take the example of utility companies. For decades, utility companies have been considered among the most stable stock investments someone could make. After all, who doesn't need power? Yet with the rise of new power sources such as wind and solar, utility providers have realized that they either must innovate and embrace these new sources or fall behind.

Every decade, year, or even month, new innovations and practices foster new opportunities. Start-up companies seize on these opportunities to create a fast growth trajectory. So can larger or longer-standing organizations. In any type of organization, it comes down to smart, tactically-aware people who are looking for inspiration

Real estate agencies over the past fifteen years are a good industry to examine as a reference for this concept. In 1999, the Internet was still the Wild Wild West. It had made and lost fortunes for many, but most smaller businesses hadn't yet jumped on the train. In the early 2000s, a number of agencies across the U.S. started to invest heavily in an online presence. A good website not only allowed potential home buyers to see new properties and listings, but with the rise of the search engines, these early players enjoyed strong search engine rankings, which translated into new business. Many of those early agencies still see those strong rankings today, where as it would cost a new entrant hundreds of thousands of dollars and much time to get to those same levels. These small business owners took a risk when they saw the opportunity, innovated, and profited immensely. Since 2010, the rise of smartphones and mobile apps has yet again changed the landscape in how people find and access home listing information and interact with real estate agencies. Yet another opportunity that presented itself to those paying attention.

To arrive at a framework for innovating, you may find the following steps useful:

1) Think about ways to improve or generate new ideas by yourself first.
2) Solicit ideas from peers, bosses, mentors, and customers.
3) Research what competitors and analogues in other industries are doing. Also, pay attention to new trends that can change your organization or industry.
4) Combine 1, 2, & 3 into innovative ideas.

You can just do steps 2 and 3, but then you don't train yourself to think up original solutions first. All of the above combine to create effective tactical thinking; an understanding of the current situation and opportunities, your current role, and your ability to pivot into new ones.

Section Four: Maximizing Opportunities – People & Relationships

Relationships are critical to succeeding professionally. You can be an unparalleled tactical genius, but you will still need money, resources, and connections to achieve your goals. All of these things stem from good relationships you create with co-workers, partners, customers, and investors.

Until or unless you see it happen in front of your eyes, most of us don't realize how many million and billion dollar decisions are made on a shake of hand between two business owners who know each other well. The details come later, executed by the various teams on both sides. One company can struggle for years to get its products in stores, while another gets its product into stores in the first month because its CEO knows the right people.

Relationship-building is how the world works. If you believe that the better product or service always wins, you are wrong. The reality is that relationships are what often make the sale or close the deal. That is what allows even mediocre organizations to keep existing. They rely on historic relationships with other organizations and have no interest in changing the status quo. The best people and the best organizations combine strong relationship-building with a great product or service. Those are the ones who succeed big.

It is your relationships with people that will help you find quicker and better paths to success.

Chapter 11: Managing Expectations

Managing expectations is an incredibly critical concept to understand and practice. It occurs in two primary ways:

- You manage expectations with others regarding due dates and timelines for any work or projects you perform and commit to.
- You manage other's expectations on the actual deliverables or outcomes of work or projects tied to you or on which you are communicating.

At its heart, the concept is simple, but in execution, it is more complex. Managing expectations well means understanding every facet of not only what you do, but also having a firm grasp on other's people work and their requirements to produce work.

Often we are overconfident in promising something. That is problematic as it causes a chain reaction when we fail to deliver. When you miss a deadline with your boss, that may cause him or her to miss a deadline with his or her boss in turn, or a customer.

When your contribution is the only factor in delivering on a promised deadline or with a certain end-result, it comes down to you. Have you done the task before, do you have the time, and have you accounted for any wild cards that might arise?

When you work within a team and / or multiple persons are contributing to a final product, you need to not only know your side of things, but also assess whether others can reliably deliver within the desired boundaries or parameters. The better you get at projecting when something can be done, in addition to the quality of that end result, the more you can manage expectations. Helpful tips:

- Become aware of how long it takes you to do certain tasks assigned to you. Get good at "guestimating" based on past experience with similar tasks or projects.

- You can always defer providing a completion date or end product until you have researched and assessed all of the variables. It is overconfidence that makes for unfeasible commitments.

- For any commitment you undertake which you haven't done before, give yourself some padding for the deadline, as well as conservatively managing expectations on the end result.

- The same holds true for tasks involving more than one person. Provide more padding the first time.

- Remember, you can always deliver faster than expected or better than expected results.

- Follow-up after making a commitment with an email or other medium that documents and confirms what you have promised to. Sometimes misunderstandings occur between what you thought you said and what the other party thought they heard. When you document it, the onus falls on the other party to have replied back with clarifications, otherwise you can point to it when you have completed the promised items.

What happens when you realize the expectations you have set are unrealistic or very difficult to meet? You have two options. First, you can speak with the other parties and change the expectations. Second option, you work the extra hours or commit the additional resources to meeting the expectations. Balance the use of both of those options. You don't want to burn through resources because you are constantly in "crisis" mode, nor do you want to establish a pattern of going back and adjusting deadlines or end deliverables.

When you fail to meet expectations, be swift in owning up to the fact and providing a new set of expectations. Your reputation relies and is built on an ability to manage expectations properly.

Chapter 12: You & Your People Skills

When you build a good reputation, people will want to work with you and you will receive a steady stream of opportunities.

Selling Yourself & Creating a Reputation

No matter what your industry, profession, or seniority level, you are your own personal salesperson. The more you communicate your strengths and engage with other professionals to recognize those strengths, the further ahead you will get. You can be a genius contributor, but if you fail to effectively promote that genius to a peer or a boss, it will go unrecognized for either much longer than it should, or forever.

Even worse is when you know someone else with skills or results worse than your own, who gets ahead of you because he or she has been able to sell themselves and their results (despite them being worse) to key individuals in an organization (or outside of it, such as customers). The better you sell yourself, the more opportunities you will be given. If you have portrayed yourself honestly, you will do well with the opportunities provided and the cycle will reinforce itself: you can showcase even more accomplishments which in turn lead to more opportunities.

Part of selling yourself revolves around being a good communicator, not only one-on-one, but also with groups of people.

What are you selling?

- Achievements. (End results as well as the methods by which you accomplished them.)
- Leadership ability and other soft skills.
- Personality traits.

- Reputation and an ability to manage expectations.
- Knowledge of your weaknesses and the work done to minimize them.

When are you selling yourself?

- The obvious: during individual and group meetings or during formal reviews.
- The not so obvious: casual conversations with your boss, other senior people in an organization, and your peers.

You have to be aware that every action you take and word you speak builds into your reputation.

How are you selling yourself?

- Do what you say you will do.
- Don't embellish your abilities or timelines.

This goes back to managing expectations. Almost all organizations will prefer someone who gets many singles consistently versus someone who gets some home runs, but strikes out most of the rest of the time.

Your reputation sells you before you even get into the room. A good reputation gives you opportunities, as it means that you can gain trust and goodwill from people who haven't worked with you or more trust from those with whom you have worked with previously.

Don't oversell what you have done or your contribution. Be straightforward. People will check and you will burn your reputation if they find out that you exaggerated your part. Don't brag about your accomplishments over and over, either. The people who tell the same "glorious" story over and over are usually the ones who only have that one story or success to point to. If you are regularly achieving results, make sure you vary the stories. Your listeners – peers and supervisors – will remember the big successes after the first time or two. Otherwise tell them about new smaller results.

Very closely related to not overselling, don't forget to be honest about your failures as well. No one is perfect, but many people gloss over their mistakes, either completely, or they sugarcoat their failures to make themselves look better. Everyone has a weakness, everyone makes mistakes. If you come across too perfect, it creates a conscious or unconscious unease in people. This can be a particularly hard lesson to understand, that talking about your mistakes actually benefits you more than pretending to be some perfect person. Acknowledge your mistakes and share what you learned from them or how you turned them into positives later.

Image

Part of selling yourself is your image. Image is the way you come across physically – in your dress, mannerisms, and physical appearance – as well as the way you communicate. The image you want to maintain and the image that the professional world finds to be acceptable often come together to influence first impressions and assumptions.

Is it unfortunate that people make assumptions before they get to know you? Of course it is. Fight those assumptions by proving them wrong with your actions, but don't feed into assumptions either. Adopt an attitude of "if it doesn't hurt me, and it probably helps, why not do it and get the possible benefits?"

You are selling yourself all the time. Understand that, practice the skills to do it well, and don't overdo it.

Empathy

Empathy is a hard skill to develop, but a huge asset if you get good at it. Empathy is the art of understanding what another person is thinking and feeling. Some people are naturally empathetic. For others it takes a commitment to gain this skill. There is some relationship to how self-centered you are and how empathetic you will therefore be.

Being able to put yourself into the mind of the other person is invaluable in communicating and managing expectations within your organization (your peers, supervisors, and reports) and with customer interaction (relationship-building, negotiating). Unpacking that a bit more:

Day-to-day communications and relationships. As an example, George takes part in a weekly team meeting of ten or so people. Every meeting, George, who probably thinks he is smarter than everyone else in the room, throws out his ideas about a topic or problem. That in and of itself is fine. But George doesn't care to hear other people's ideas or contributions; he is dismissive of all of them. It's his way or the highway. Guess what? Everyone either secretly or openly hates George. George doesn't realize this though. Because he believes himself to be so smart, he assumes everyone else believes he is smart and likes him because of that. He lacks the ability to empathize, to put himself in his co-workers' shoes who are all thinking, "George is not a nice fellow, not a team player." George is probably surprised when his boss brings it up at some point: "What do you mean? Most of the team is frustrated with me?" People like George are – unfortunately - incredibly common. There are various degrees of this type of behavior. Do you have to agree with someone all of the time or cave in even when you have a good point? Of course not. But understand the other person's perspective. At the very least, it helps you to craft counter-arguments.

Customer / client interactions. You will have considerable success if you can put yourself in a customer's shoes and understand their current problems, how they think about those problems, and what solutions they are looking for. If you know these things and communicate them well, you will develop deep, long relationships, not simply a one-time sale or service.

Unlike anticipation, which uses past actions to think about future actions, empathy focuses on figuring out what someone is thinking now and why. Here is a good way to learn to empathize:

- Listen carefully to those around you when they make major points and statements. Then ask yourself what is motivating them to say that or take that stance?
- Watch how people react when you say something and try to understand what they are thinking when you say it.
- Ask yourself two questions when speaking with others: "what would I want to hear in that situation?" and "what would I think is fair if I was in that situation?"

The biggest strength of empathy is gaining a level of insight into others that allows you to craft your words and actions to build a shared stance with them.

Don't confuse empathy with weakness. Understanding the other side does not mean that you have to accommodate them. You are finding ways through empathy to avoid roadblocks and make advancements.

Assessing People

You will meet a lot of people in your life. Some are positive influences, some negative. Some help your career, while others hinder it. Do you make your own opinions on others? Here's a sample scenario:

Beth starts a new job, and during lunch on the first day, sits down with a colleague. The colleague tells Beth, "So I would avoid John if I were you. John is hard to work with and you should take what he says with a grain of salt." Beth suddenly has a very negative opinion about John. Is that right?

No! Don't take opinions, negative or positive about others at face value until you have made a judgment yourself. There could be a hundred reasons that Beth dislikes John, which may have nothing to do with John's work or his overall interaction with his colleagues. Or, John could have done one thing wrong and Beth is the type of person that blows it out of proportion. Maybe Beth is afraid that you working with John will undermine her position. Maybe Beth's personality is the issue if she enjoys spreading gossip. You just don't know.

Trust very few people's opinions of others. Most men and women aren't good at providing an unbiased, fair assessment of a person's capabilities. Even when you hear an assessment from someone you trust, dig if possible to verify. Wait until you personally talk to someone to start forming your opinion and reserve full judgment until you have also seen that person's work.

On another point, some folks just consistently say the wrong thing, lacking political savvy or common sense. But they may still do excellent work. Everyone has weaknesses or deficits, you need to understand them, plan for them, and therefore not let them interfere with your own work or goals.

Even when you do find issues with someone, there typically are ways to work around them if you must continue to interact with that person. Double-checking work, ensuring conversations take place in front of a superior, etc. These are not ideal solutions, but you will never have a perfect workplace with no issues. Even the best people have highs and lows because of changes professionally or personally. Accept that fact and learn to deal with these types of situations.

You know your own strengths and weaknesses. Grow your knowledge of others' strengths and weaknesses. Learn whom you can depend on, and when.

Learning the Office "Game"

No one really enjoys office politics. The term itself has a negative connotation. So let's call it the office "game". We would all rather do our work well, enjoy it as much as possible, and be confident in the fact that our work will stand on its merits independently. In reality, your reputation and the perceptions that others share about you matter quite a bit. People with bad intent can and do spread gossip and half-truths, much of which is never said directly to you, but spoken about behind your back. Your work is judged on what people have heard about you as much (or sometimes more than) the work itself. People suck-up to bosses and other figures of authority to try and curry favors and get their way. All of these sorts of things are part of the office game.

If you can escape these types of antics completely, do so. If you can't, learn how to navigate the waters, so you don't get bogged down in the office game unknowingly. Every organization larger than one person, regardless of size, origin, or industry, plays the office game to some degree.

Replace all mentions of professional life and organizations with "personal life" and "family" and you suddenly realize we play a very similar game in our personal lives. If you become good at the office game, you will have an immensely powerful leg up on 90% (some would say 99%) of other people in the organization.

How do you learn to play the office game? With diplomacy. Don't undermine people; stay above negative developments in the workplace. You will always be worse off for getting sucked into drama or plotting. Avoid the negative elements and be a positive force in the office. Do to so however requires that you comprehend how the forces of the office game work:

- How one person connects to another in the organization. including which people in the organization have long-standing ties to managers.
- Which people don't seem to get penalized for poor work or missed deadlines, and why.
- What someone's professional and personal stakes are in the task, project, or organization.

- How much time and energy they have invested in a task or project.
- How others react to what you say.
- What others do when they feel insulted or slighted.
- Who acts differently (negatively) when the boss isn't around.
- Who solves problems and who creates them.
- Which people make the various types of pertinent decisions in the organization.
- What others actually think of you (versus what they say to you).

Some of these things come from observation, some from talking to others and getting their opinions. Listen and figure out where you can enact positive approaches. If you do this regularly, you will learn:

- How to phrase things more tactfully to each situation.
- When to be aggressive, and when to wait patiently.
- When not to say anything, and when not to engage.
- When and how to take issues or ideas to your peers directly and when instead to take them to supervisors or other managers.
- Which people to speak to with issues or ideas.
- Which people to avoid as much as possible.

Perhaps the best analogy is that while most people play checkers, you should instead play chess. Become aware of all of the interpersonal elements swirling around all of the tasks and projects that must be carried out, and you will grasp how to best leverage and work with people to get those tasks done well.

Chapter 13: Building Relationships & Networks

Many people emphasize the importance of networking: "You should network, it will help your career". You aren't an army of one; even one-person organizations have customers, partners, someone. The more people you know, the better.

Networking and building relationships are not the same thing. Anyone can "network" at a lunch or an event and get business cards or shake a hand. Few of those names will turn into substantive relationships that drive friendships and / or business, and it takes an applied effort to do so.

There are three types of networkers:

- Those who network and build relationships naturally.
- Those who have to make a conscious effort to network.
- Those who don't understand the importance of building relationships.

To break to the first-person for a moment, I fell into that third group of people for a long time. I thought that I could rely only on my own intelligence, ideas, and abilities to lead me to success. Not because I thought others weren't as good as me, but because I grew up not relying on others and taking pride in making my own way. I had enough friends, but missed many opportunities where I met amazing people and didn't make an effort to foster deeper relationships.

The benefits of having a strong and deep professional network are that it:

- Builds your credibility and reputation.
- Creates regular opportunities through word-of-mouth.
- Teaches you new skills.
- Opens up chances for partnerships and new initiatives.

Your old biology teacher? She knows the best employer in town and may get you a job. The executive you met at a conference? He remembered your insightful questions and wants you on his team. Your friend's roommate? Amazing programmer that helps you build a website.

Make honest, deep relationships naturally and augment that with strategic networking, both in-person and digitally. Broaden your network through professional events and conferences, spending time socializing with work colleagues as well as connecting through mediums such as LinkedIn and associations that cater to your particular field or profession.

What is a good gauge to know if you are on the right track? By the time you are three years into your career, here are a few indicators of a good professional network:

- Have at least 500 connections on LinkedIn.
- Meet at least ten new people each month.
- Have a Board of Mentors (two to five) who are senior in their careers / industries, to whom you can (and do) casually turn to for advice.
- Keep up with your network by sending regular updates and thoughts (social networks have made this incredibly easy to do).
- Have the ability to call upon three senior references.
- Be able to call upon five peer references.

There is a perception that it is difficult to network with "successful" people. Yes, they are busy, but almost all of them are also interested in mentoring others to succeed. These men and women regularly say, "feel free to reach out to me for advice", yet few people actually reach out, notably the younger ones who are either anxious or don't realize the opportunity. You should be proactive in reaching out to successful people. Be honest, show a willingness to learn, and you will find plenty of them to help guide you on your path.

Don't network only with seniors (mentors) and your peers. Also take the time to network with your juniors; they too will grow in stature and helpfulness. They may be great candidates to join your team one day, or perhaps their careers put them in a position where you end up working for them.

Networking Inside of Your Organization

The notion of intra-company networking is often overlooked but incredibly valuable.

Communication is a fundamental aspect of networking and building your reputation, part of your personal salesmanship. You shouldn't be content to do your job well without anyone knowing you are doing it well! You also don't want your reputation to rely on the word of a single person - most often a boss or supervisor - as so many men and women tend to do. There isn't anything wrong, of course, with your boss knowing you do a good job, but what happens when he or she leaves the organization? Takes an extended vacation? Do you think that your boss makes compensation and salary decisions alone? (Hint: most supervisors don't; they either get final approvals from *their* bosses, or decisions are made by a group / committee.)

What if a promising new position opened up internally in your organization? Would you get it if you deserved it? One of the worse things that can happen is when you plan on applying for or working toward another position, and it ends up goes to someone else less qualified. Often it isn't that a manager made a consciously bad decision, it is that they weren't aware of your interest, your talents, or even you in general. In those cases, it is your partly fault that you didn't network enough and sell yourself.

The art - and it is an art - of internal networking, revolves around a reputation that screams "trust". It gives you an initial level of credibility with others in an organization. Your reputation should be built on well-managed expectations, backed by strong results.

Do you know which people in the organization make the primary strategic and personnel decisions? It is a smaller group than most think. Are you known to those people?

Have you identified other rising stars in the organization? It is a time-honored premise for success. The man or woman who climbs three or four levels in an organization in fast succession doesn't do so without help and support. Forming a close, mutually-beneficial relationship with such rising star will likely produce a faster career track and many more opportunities than normal. Find the stars in your organization.

Everyone matters in an organization in their own way. Don't wrongly assume here that you should ignore "non-key" people. In a well-run organization, every person holds an important role, and every person can help you in your career, as you in turn can help them.

Learn about people, learn how to interact with them, build deep relationships with them.

Section Five: Skills for Success

There are some skills that are pretty universally helpful in your career, in any field or industry. This section covers those skills. What it doesn't cover are skills specific to your field or profession, also known as technical skills. There are thousands and thousands of types of technical skills, and as such, they go well beyond the scope here. It is enough to say:

- Have honest, regular assessments of the level of your technical skills.
- Strive to be, at first, the best in your organization, then the best among your competitors, and then you can reach for being the best in your industry and beyond.
- Either improve deficits in your skills or find ways to reduce them as weaknesses by collaboration or developing parallel skills.

Chapter 14: Public Speaking & Presentations

Is public speaking an art or a science? There exist naturally gifted speakers, but public speaking is a very learnable skill. The art of speaking in front of groups of people is a critical part of communicating points and sharing ideas. Unless you plan to run for public office, you don't need to learn to speak in front of thousands of people, though the skills to speak in front of twenty people are much the same as speaking to two-hundred or two-thousand. It doesn't require an extroverted personality, speaking for hours, or learning a set formula that keeps your audience happy 10% of the time and somber 5% of the time.

Think of every public speaker to whom you have ever listened; some are quiet and reserved, some are loud and boisterous. They can smile the whole time and still bore their audience to death, or they can be serious and somber and yet keep everyone on the edge of their seats. Just like Hollywood actors, there are a range of styles, but the best public speakers all share the same ability to clearly and effectively engage *with* their audiences.

Do you hate speaking in front of others or don't think it is one of your strengths? Welcome to the club. Even the most experienced speakers have some stage fright. It is what helps them stay sharp and practiced.

Good public speaking is really the art of storytelling. Imagine one of your favorite books or movies. Now remove all of the descriptions, embellishments, special effects, and tangents authors and producers take us on (and which are ever so great to read or watch). A good story, even devoid of all of those elements, will still have a compelling path from beginning to end that engages the audience. Improv is where you make up stories live in front of a group; public speaking is planned. The best stories flow amazingly well. They are elegant in their simplicity, which is high praise indeed for the immense amount of work that goes into them. Once you begin thinking of public speaking as storytelling, with clear ways of construction, you will stop thinking of it as an arcane art and instead view it as a learnable skill.

Create the Story

As a storyteller, regardless of the length of time you intend to speak, two minutes or twenty, the following rules apply:

1) Develop a story *for the audience* you are speaking to, not just a string of everything *you* want to say on a subject.
2) The story must be framed with and use the lexicon of your audience. Don't create a technical-jargon-laced story for a non-technical audience.
3) Create a clear story with a beginning, middle, and end.
4) The beginning of the beginning, known as the introduction, is where you tell your audience what you are going to speak about.
5) Spend the rest of the speech, until the end, telling them what you promised to tell them.
6) End with a summary of what you told them.
7) Your speech should have at least one key point, or peak.
8) Longer speeches with several subjects or elements have multiple peaks, one per each section.
9) Write down each point in one or two sentences. Almost any subject on earth can be boiled down to a single sentence. It is like writing a long paper in high school or college. Your thesis sentence is the distillation and primary point of the entire paper.
10) With each new section, ensure that you have a set of points that build to your key statement, your peak.
11) Build to the peaks in each section. Imagine a series of valleys and peaks that keep your audience flowing through differing levels of energy.
12) Link the different subjects / elements together with transitions.

13) If you can't link the different subjects together, it is a sign that you shouldn't be including everything in one speech.

14) Refine the story. Every first draft can use refining. Not only adding, but also subtracting secondary elements or things that don't further your main point(s).

15) The more broadly uninteresting your material, the more you need to hone it down.

16) You are done. You have a good speech. <u>Everything else is optional</u>.

Remember, if you can't link the different subjects together, it is a sign that you shouldn't be including everything in one speech.

Sound too easy? Or do these steps seem like a lot? Looking for the additional guidelines about inserting embellishments, jokes, or another complex framework? Not necessary! Of all of the speeches and presentations out there, only a small handful have a good story framework. Some others are still engaging because of the speaker's charisma or perhaps because of funny jokes thrown in. But all of those additional elements are secondary. If you weave a good core story, your audience will be engaged, you will make your points well, and you don't need to add anything else. If you want to, and as your public speaking skills grow, by all means throw in those witty analogies, but get the core methodology down first, as that is the part that really matters.

Even when you are talking about a subject that many people find pretty boring, the rules apply. In fact, the rules apply even more strongly as you need to have that much more of a well-crafted story to keep your audience engaged. For example, an IT person needs to discuss an upcoming email and server migration process with various members of the organization, some of whom are technical, some not. Not a topic that 99% of people would willingly sit through. Most of these types of IT speeches make watching paint dry sound like a party. (IT folks, sorry for picking on you, but you make a great example.) The IT person goes slide by slide in his presentation, with loose organization, weighing each sentence as much (or as little) as the one before it. There is no story; it is just a large amount of facts that go on for twenty minutes. Worst of all, it is so boring that most people forget the few pertinent facts in the speech amongst all of the secondary noise. Bleh. On the other hand, the same type of material can be delivered to the same types of managers, in half the time, in a story form, where the speaker engages with his or her listeners, keeps them interested, and the audience walks away feeling informed and energetic.

Learn To Tell the Story

Now that you have your story, you must figure out how to tell it. These tips have less of a required order:

- Learn your material inside and out. The more you know your material, the more confident and less nervous you will be. You will greatly reduce filler words and avoid stuttering.
- Practice, practice, practice before the official speech.
- Practice in front of the mirror.
- Record yourself speaking and play it back.
- Practice in front of your friend or loved one.
- Practice in front of your co-workers.
- Practice individual sections out of order for longer speeches, instead of working beginning to end every time.
- As you learn your material, and you have practiced it many times, then you can worry about the more advanced nuances of public speaking.

(All further points below are more optional. Knowledge of your material and confidence are the critical factors.)

- Pay attention to stutters, repetition, filler words such as "um", "uh", "like", and "so", and repeating favored phrases too much (done unconsciously most of the time).
- Listen to your rhythm (the pace at which you speak as well as use pauses for effect), tone, and confidence.
- Move your attention across your audience (if in person), stopping to look some people in the eyes at key points you wish to engage them with, but otherwise looking slightly above the eyes (foreheads are a good focal point) to eliminate your anxiety. To most listeners, it will still seem as if you are looking into their eyes.
- Watch your physical gestures, posture, and general body movement, if speaking in person. The more you control and use your hands properly to emphasize, the more compelling you will be.

- Begin naturally adding in analogies, jokes, and other embellishments. You will get a feel for doing this as you speak to groups more frequently and you become comfortable with the material.

You have crafted the story, and you have learned to tell it. This is really 99% of the work required to be a good group speaker. If you are still nervous, there are many tricks to reducing the feeling – a common one is to imagine your audience naked – but these are all secondary to a good story that you know inside and out. That is what best builds confidence and eliminates nervousness.

Informal vs. Formal Speaking

Much of the ability (or lack thereof) of public speaking is psychological. Steve might be a thoughtful, inspirational speaker around the lunch table with his peers, but when he goes in front of his bosses, he freezes up and stutters. It's a common phenomenon where men and women overthink the concept of speaking in more formal settings, and trip over themselves. Take your favorite hobby or passion: you could tell someone an engaging story without even thinking through the process of creating it. We speak with our friends and loved ones all of the time. More formal speaking is the same thing if you learn the story and practice it.

Grow your speaking skills every day by incorporating these practices in even the smallest of group settings. Before a meeting with team members, you might do one or all of the below:

- Spend two minutes writing bullet points on the main topics you want to get across when you speak and on how to actively link those topics together to create the story.
- Listen to yourself speak to try and catch weak points and unclear phrasing. Also watch gestures and mannerisms.
- Constantly watch other people who speak in the group. How do they use their hands? How often do they say the word "like" or "so", etc.? How do they take their topics and speak about them in a way that is clear and compelling?

Instead of practicing intensively only for those "big" but more infrequent opportunities or obligations, practice more constantly for the smaller ones as well and you will build experience quickly. At the end of the day, if you can become a good storyteller in the first couple of years of your professional career, you will surpass many people who are five, ten, or twenty years your senior in that very critical area of effective communication. You will be seen as an authority on the topics you speak on, you will be noticed, and you will get ahead.

Packaging Information

The best communicators out there, the ones who build real trust with their audience, are those who talk *with* their listeners, not *at* them. This means packaging and delivering the content – of an email, phone call, meeting, lecture, etc. – into clusters of information that the audience can digest.

No one likes being talked down to, no one. Related to this notion, most people will not admit ignorance. They will not ask questions about something they don't understand, as they don't want to be seen as slow or unknowledgeable. Or, if you introduce too many facts or figures into your dialogue / presentation, your audience may start to nitpick on a few elements that they do somewhat understand, derailing you from getting your main points across.

If you are presenting to a group of people who are really quantitative – who like fancy numbers and charts - give that to them. If you have a group that is more visual, craft the material that way. But whether you go for the numbers or a more qualitative flow of information, don't make something unnecessarily complex. Your ability to take a complex topic and make it accessible to any audience is a sign of your mastery and understanding of that topic. You can always throw in fancy logic, charts, calculations, and metrics. But if you need to utilize all of that to explain your point (e.g., presenting to a group of senior leaders why you should enact a new process), you will often lose them during the course of that explanation versus boiling down your information to refined points.

Time and time again, this approach of boiling down complex information will yield many gains. Your credibility rises especially when others (including any of your predecessors) have always portrayed a particular point or topic as arcane or requiring a "genius" to understand. When you simplify it down to its core elements, you will be seen as smart, sharp, and relatable.

Decisions are not made in a vacuum. Smaller decisions might only go through your team, while the larger ones may be vetted by your superiors in the organization. At all levels, your ability to paint a clear picture of a possible direction is crucial to getting buy-in, sign-off, and participation, whether that be during a five-minute phone call or a two-hour formal presentation. To make even the complex clear:

- Learn to condense every topic or strategy you wish to cover into three or four distinct points.
- Ensure you have removed overly complex information as well as shorthand or technical references that make the conversation less accessible.
- Create a clear picture of the historical / present status (if applicable) versus your proposal for the future. Make it very simple and clear as to why what you are proposing is better.

Visual Presentations

If you have some sort of visual material that accompanies your speech, here are some best practices:

- **Learn your material still!** When you simply read off of the slides instead of engaging with the audience, you get bored and the audiences gets bored.
- **Don't put a lot of written content on your presentation / slides**. Your audience will read the material instead of listening to you. Even if you are going to be speaking to a group with a limited amount of time and patience, make your visual aids short and sweet. Some presenters think to themselves, "Well, the detailed handout I produce will provide content for those who want to skip ahead or move at their own pace." Bad idea for a presentation. Detailed handouts for the "advanced" listeners will often only cause them to ask more in-depth questions as they work through the presentation, ignoring your planned sequence of events.
- **Leverage the benefits of visual information to display complex data in charts, tables, and graphs.** An elegant

chart will hammer home the point as you talk about it. A nice table will organize important information much more precisely than your gestures. For most audiences, hearing number after number just makes them all blur together.

- **Stay away from fancy animations or gimmicky pictures.** Enough said. Be clean and classy.
- **Sequence your visual aids in a way that complements the story you have created.** Build to key points, then ebb, then again come back to key points. Think carefully on where you want your best visual aids to engage the audience or reinforce a point.

Non-Verbal Reports & Presentations

Any report or fact-set that you are not verbalizing requires as much care as a spoken presentation. Here, you fill in the supplemental detail you would otherwise be speaking to. But you must still craft a story with good flow, clarity, and logic. Pretty much every guideline laid out above for speaking to groups holds true. Long rambling reports won't be read by many, so condense them down to the essential points.

Master the art of storytelling. Almost everything you do is some form of a story about yourself, your experiences, your team, your products, or your organization. Do yourself the justice of telling those stories well.

Chapter 15: Time & Communication Management

The busier you get, the more time becomes a precious commodity. The busier you get, the more critical it is to communicate clearly and effectively.

Time Management

Organize your time. To-do lists are a must. More than just making a simple list, prioritize tasks that need to get done. Accomplishing everything on your to-do list often feels impossible. Working chronologically through your to-do list doesn't solve the issue, as more tasks arrive continuously. Use the 80 / 20 rule constantly: figure out which 20% of your tasks will produce 80% of the results. Not all tasks are equal, and good time management translates better to effective project management, where you must balance not only your own time, but others' time as well.

Follow priorities in communication. Ask those who work with you to call or speak with you face-to-face if something is urgent. Email can wait. Checking email can be a compulsion, but experiment with the notion of checking email only once an hour for a dedicated amount of time, then switching back to working on other things. If anything major happens, someone can call you.

Set aside quiet work time. Identify quiet blocks (typically early in the day or in the evening) when you don't have emails pouring in or others interrupting you. Those will be your most productive times, often also the times you can do the most thinking. During the rest of the day, give yourself blocks of time for each task and try to get it done.

Create shorter deadlines. On larger projects or activities, give yourself shorter deadlines that you can achieve and feel good about. Especially with projects that take days, weeks, or months to complete, make small wins for yourself. You will find yourself managing your time that much better.

Organize thoughts before phone calls and meetings. With so many things going on, we often run into meetings or start phone calls without having planned out what we are going to say; it is mostly improv. Avoid this by developing a habit of spending two minutes before a phone call or meeting thinking about what you want to say and how you want to say it.

Set aside time to relax. Don't forget to take time to completely unhook, unwind, and relax. We now live in such a constantly plugged-in world, that we forget or feel unable to step back. Free time and vacations are even more important in your professional life than during high school or college. Do your work well, put all of your attention and focus into that work, and then when you have finished, stop completely. That can be hard when you are engaged with your work or want to make that extra bit of money. But you will wear yourself down, bit by bit, day by day. You will feel the effects not only in your overall productivity, but also in your creative thinking. The best notions come most frequently when our minds unwind.

Communication Mediums & Tips

Each method of communicating has pluses and minuses. Figure out which ones work best for you and your team. Some tips for each medium follow.

Meetings:

- **Eliminate all non-necessary scheduled meetings.** How many standing weekly or monthly meetings and phone calls do you have? Before you know it, you have five, then six, then seven meetings a week during fixed periods that all take thirty to sixty minutes and eat up a lot of your day. Multiply that out by all of the attendees and you are talking about a lot of resources eaten up by meetings. Test the value of a specific meeting by reducing its frequency to once every other period, or merging it with another meeting. After a good meeting, you should walk away with finite next steps or new things learned. If you aren't, the meeting is not a productive use of time and should be changed and eliminated.

- **Keep meetings small.** Meetings with too many people waste most people's time. Few contribute and the rest simply listen or don't listen and do something else. Include the main people that must be there and rely on them to relay information to their teams or peers after the meeting concludes.
- **Meet ad hoc for specific issues.** Instead of only scheduled meetings where most of the time is spent recounting what everyone has done, use meetings to get very specific things done, and then conclude the meeting. These are sometime called "blitz" meetings because they occur and conclude so suddenly to achieve a single goal.

Email:

- **Bullet Points**. Use bullet points or numbered lists to keep points distinct and make the email easier to read, notably when you write longer or complex emails.
- **Email subjects**. Change / rename the subject if your email thread switches topics.
- **Length of emails**. Long emails should be written only to document something in writing or work through complex topics. Even then, phone calls or meetings are typically better.
- **Many people on the email.** If you anticipate a lot of back-and-forth or have many parties in the email thread that are all going to be responding, have a conference call or meeting instead.

Phone:

The tips on meetings apply. The only other note: learn to enjoy talking about the weather. It is the most common way of starting a phone conversation between people in different geographic areas.

Texting:

This method of communication hasn't been around very long and was once the domain only of teens and young adults. No longer. Texting in the business world has blossomed on all levels. Senior managers who are in their 50s and 60s text. There's a good reason for it. Texting boils down conversations to short, clear questions and answers. Answers that require more space can be taken to the phone, but you can convey information quickly and conduct rapid back-and-forth dialogues with multiple people. If you do like to text:

- Wait for your boss or other managers to initiate the text, as there are still many people who find it too informal and dislike its use. As long as you are taking cues though from a senior person, you are fine.
- Don't use emoticons or informal terms like "u" instead of "you". Keep it business professional.

Use your time wisely and communicate effectively. There are only so many hours in the day. Treat everything like it is a valuable commodity and you will make wiser decisions.

Chapter 16: Numbers, Spreadsheets, & Budgeting

Not everyone likes numbers. However, while you don't have to know calculus, all organizations use some basic number manipulation on things like sales, donor estimates, project costs, or resource allocations. Even if you hate numbers, learn to work with them effectively, as they allow you greater input into dictating courses of events in responsibilities and projects.

If you learn nothing else, at least know the key metrics and figures that you, your team, and your organization are measured on. They could simply be time-based goals, or they might be tied to sales, costs, or productivity. The more you know these values, why they matter, and how to use them, the more you will be able to speak on the same level with senior team members or your boss.

Spreadsheets

If you truly feel like you have no need for spreadsheets in your professional career, skip this part.

Spreadsheets have been around for a long time now. It would likely amaze you as to how many multi-billion dollar companies - despite their purchases of $100,000 dedicated software and systems - still use spreadsheets. Spreadsheets have upper limits as to what they can do, but those upper limits are fairly high. It is actually the ease and speed with which spreadsheets can be deployed that has kept them so relevant.

Spreadsheets are one of the few "universal" skillsets mentioned here as they have a large amount of value relative to the time spent learning to use them. They are highly useful for everything from creating complex schedules and project plans, to data sorting, key metrics calculation, and sophisticated data analysis. At their most basic, they create very effective visual tables.

If you want a quickly organized table on the status and various metrics of 15 or 20 projects, a spreadsheet table will serve you well as you can re-order and re-organize very quickly. With other document types, this information sits in bullet points or paragraphs of text, and cannot be manipulated as easily.

You can find exact spreadsheet formulas for yourself online or through other resources. These skills can be picked up with a few weeks of dedicated practice, or a few months of intermittent practice. Learn to do all of these elements as a base:

- Creating schedules and tables of information organized into columns and rows.
- Applying filters to organize and sift through information.
- Using basic mathematical formulas (adding, subtracting, multiplying, dividing).
- Dragging and copying formulas across multiple cells. (Invaluable in letting you make fast updates across a larger amount of data.)
- Leveraging Pivot tables (© Excel) for fast manipulation of data sets by time or by a desired category.
- Cleaning and standardizing data.
- Joining different data sets together with matching formulas.

Anything more sophisticated really just builds on the above elements, and with "only" the above, you will be able to scan through and look at data in different ways to make analytical decisions.

Budgets

Don't worry, this isn't a book on accounting. You can explore that on your own. Most positions benefit highly from an awareness of how budgets work and how to budget in an organizational setting. That benefit changes to a necessity as soon as you gain more formal supervision over a project and / or a team. You don't need to learn cash flow formulas, understand taxes, or any other higher financial-level detail (unless you are in finance or getting into a role that demands it).

Good project budgets are put together based on:

- A team or organization's existing resources: labor and time available to get a project completed.
- Expenditures required in excess of existing resources: hiring more people and spending additional money on materials, tools, or any other third parties.
- Expected outcome and / or ROI (return on invested dollars or time).

To fashion a budget, you need to have a firm grasp of your abilities and time requirements, others' abilities and time requirements, and where you have resource gaps that require filling. To do this:

1) Identify every person / team that needs to help with the project.
2) Work with them to calculate the amount of time they will require to complete their portion. Some organizations don't care about tracking time by projects, others like to because it gives them a sense of where time has been used productively. (But that is a finance department function in most cases).
3) Isolate the areas wherein the project requires external resources, such as contractors or vendors.
4) Find the costs of all third party contractors and vendors for the project. (Try to have someone with experience do this, as you will otherwise highly increase the chances of underestimating the time and / or money required).
5) Pinpoint all of the materials, non-human resources, and tools that you need to purchase.
6) Categorize the costs for those materials, non-human resources, and tools.

Now you just have to put it all together:

1) Create a table with columns for every time period (days, weeks, months, or quarters).

2) The first section of rows will be your internal staff and resources. Put in hours spent per period (or actual cost per person).

3) The second section of rows will be your external contractors and vendors. Put in their cost per each time period.

4) The third section lists all non-human resources. Put costs into the time period during which you will incur them.

5) Total everything up.

To see an example of a budget in complete table form, check out http://www.succeedbig.com/budget-table .

There is not any complex math here. It is more about putting pieces together in an organized way. You can spend time making the table more aesthetically appealing, but you've just created a functional budget. Nice work.

Section Six: Stepping Back: Career Evaluation & Options

Time flies. It is important to step back regularly and evaluate where you are versus where you planned to be and where you want to go next. This section deals with making a proper evaluation of your current status, the various options you have for change, and how to best transition out of your current organization.

Chapter 17: Assessing Your Current Situation

Every three or six months you should take a few hours of solitude and reflect on your current situation. What has changed in the last few months and do any of those changes - positive or negative - mean you need or want to consider a change? It may seem like a small thing to set aside that time, but amid everything else that occupies your schedule, it gets overlooked.

Where are you right now and what factors might you be considering? Are you happy where you are? Do you feel as if you have been making progress professionally? Or are you starting to feel unhappy and considering a change? Common reasons people have for switching organizations or careers include:

- **Poor Compensation.** You didn't know average salaries when you applied, you haven't received regular salary increases with time or seniority, or you know you can make more money elsewhere.
- **Lack of Challenge / Responsibilities**. You are able and willing to do more, but your day is predictable because you learned how to do the job months and months ago. The position becomes more about counting down the hours until the end of the day, instead of being fully engaged.
- **Poor Growth Opportunity.** This is closely related the lack of challenge / responsibilities. Good performers want formal growth opportunities. Perhaps the organization doesn't have a career track that appeals to you. Or positions may only open if or when someone retires,

keeping you from executing at the level you think you are capable of. You want to keep evolving your skillsets, whether those be technical skills or soft skills.

- **Your supervisor / management of the organization.** They are poor managers, mean ones, short-sighted......take your pick. Instead of being a positive force in your life, they make it worse.
- **Your co-workers and the organizational culture.** You don't mesh well with your co-workers or the culture, making the days pretty unenjoyable. Or you feel that the organization's philosophy / mission has steadily eroded since you began working there.
- **Personal changes.** Your health, your family, your hobbies, other things that have changed.
- **A new opportunity outside of your current organization has opened up.** Something that professionally, financially, or personally appeals to you more than your current role.

One or more of the above reasons could signal a time for change. Hence the need for regular review periods around your personal and professional objectives; where you are versus where you thought you would be, and what you want to be doing next.

Things You Can't Change

In any organization, there are going to be things you can't change; elements that you don't like or that you don't agree with. Nothing is perfect for everyone. To be clear, don't sacrifice your ideals. Never sacrifice your ideals. But everyone has something to dislike about an organization.

Consciously pay attention to the things you can't change. You may have amazing ideas but the culture of the organization prevents you from being able to test them or enact them. You may dislike the way an organization treats its employees, including you. If you do learn the industry and competitors, you will also have a gauge of whether these issues are confined to only your organization or all of them. Push against these boundaries and roadblocks, see if you can work around them, and then for anything that still bothers you or seems impossible to modify, have honest conversations with yourself about whether a current opportunity is worth it, or not.

As you figure out the things you can't change, you can focus on the things that are open to improvement or new ideas. You must feel like you can make positive progress and an impact on the role you hold. Act on the things you can change.

Keep Current with Your Manager

Schedule time consistently with your manager to discuss your role and opportunities within the organization. The idea here is to have regular conversations, not a sudden confrontation because you are upset and feel like you are not progressing quickly enough. Instead of bringing up your desires or concerns suddenly during one meeting in a confrontational manner, check in with him or her regularly to gauge how they feel your development is progressing and what the next level in the organization looks like for you.

If you have a great manager, they will be having these conversations with you already as part of a planned development initiative. If not, make it happen. Sudden brain dumps on your manager with all of your pent-up feelings and issues will likely make him or her defensive. As issues or questions arise, discuss them. This approach also lets your manager know you are forward-thinking, which is always a good thing.

You of course want your boss to manage expectations properly. If they give you clear measures that you meet or exceed, and you don't get the promised results, your expectations haven't been managed well. Conversely, if you fail to meet your side of the bargain, you should be honest with yourself.

Length of Time Spent in an Organization

How much time do you spend with an organization? There isn't a single hard or fast rule. Some organizations simply aren't the fit you might have initially thought them to be. On the other hand, you don't want to create a pattern of short-tenure positions with various organizations. Many organizations - more specifically the managers and recruiters in them - will flat out ignore resumes and remove them from further consideration when they suggest a pattern of short tenures.

A lack of long tenures at previous organizations often signals one or more of the following potential problems with a candidate:

- **They are a bad egg.** Their skills are worse than they are made out to be. They can't work well with their peers or they are bad team players. They don't listen to their supervisor. They exert a negative influence or vibe in the workplace, etc. Something that resulted in them needing to leave the organization.
- **Bad luck / personal issues.** Some people just seem to have consistent bad luck, such as constant illness, or interpersonal issues that follow them from job to job.
- **They are completely self-motivated opportunists.** You should be thinking regularly about whether your current position is the best place for you personally and professionally. But getting 100% of what you want without giving 100% isn't fair or sustainable. Managers don't want to spend the time training and molding someone on their team, only for that person to leave the minute they feel they have picked up the skills they were after.

No matter how smart you are or how well-honed your professional skills, you are not going to be contributing 100% of your potential to an organization for at least a couple of months. It takes time to learn the operational dynamics of an organization (its people, opportunities, deficiencies, etc.), do your job well based on those dynamics, and work with others effectively. An organization looking to hire someone wants some degree of confidence that that person will be there for the long-term; a resume full of short-term tenures raises a lot of questions. This is all a thorough way of saying that your past actions can affect future prospects.

Those are the various pieces to consider when you make your periodic self-evaluations. At the end of the day, it isn't worth being unhappy in your position or being stuck in a rut. If you do want to succeed big professionally, you must always consider your forward momentum.

Chapter 18: Options & Considerations for Change

Here is a typical situation: the company you work for is pretty decent, your supervisor is average (not bad, not great), and you have been in the role for a little over a year-and-a-half. You know your job well, and think you do it well. The pay isn't horrible, but it isn't great either. Exclude things like changes in your personal life. At the end of the day, you are studying your options for the next phase of your career. There aren't that many choices:

1) You stay where you are... no change financially or responsibility-wise.
2) You get a promotion... with financial and / or responsibility changes.
3) You leave the organization... to get financial and / or responsibility changes.
4) You go back to school.

Each choice has positives and negatives tied to it. No choice is "wrong", but you should be making the choice very deliberately, in periods of calm reflection.

There are plenty of valid reasons to take Choice #1. Maybe the job provides a great work / life balance for you right now. Maybe you like the level of responsibility tied to the position, or the work is pretty interesting. Compensation-wise....well everyone always wants more money, but let's say you are making enough to live fairly happily. There is absolutely nothing wrong with Choice #1.

Choices #2 and #3 are more closely tied to one another. If you are not considering Choice #1, you should be weighing between

Choice #2 and Choice #3. Compare your current options in the organization against professional opportunities elsewhere, in terms of compensation and growth prospects. One element for you to consider regarding a switch in organizations: Certain things reset when you move to a new organization. Promotions in the first twelve months at a new organization are rare. The time it takes you to ramp up, the time it takes your new manager to vet your skills, and the time it takes to establish interpersonal relationships and trust often take you to the one-year mark. Would you have gotten further in your current organization in that same period?

Choice #4: Going Back to School

Should you pursue additional schooling after beginning your professional career? Like many questions in the rest of this book, it is less about an absolute right or wrong answer versus thinking through your circumstances properly and making a decision based on those circumstances.

You can really separate your decision here into just two choices.

Get the degree / certification:

- **Pros**. Increase your compensation and / or your seniority / responsibilities in organizations after you get it OR gain new skills that also help you switch roles or industries.
- **Cons**. You lose the real-life experience and compensation you would have made during your schooling period and possibly incur debt.

Don't get the degree / certification:

- **Pros**. You keep getting on-the-job experience and making money without additional debt.
- **Cons**. In some organizations, it can keep you from getting the compensation and promotion jumps you would otherwise.

Specifically regarding MBA degrees, they teach you a lot of the higher-end strategic and financial skills that most undergraduate college programs never cover. If you can learn those skills before seeking an MBA, you will get further ahead than most of your peers. If you don't have a chance or the ability to learn them early, business school may be the perfect place.

Moving to another industry or type of role is often a great reason to pursue another degree that imparts on you the knowledge and skills for that new area. If you majored in history in college, perhaps you decide an MBA is the best way of gaining a clear set of skills and certifications that set you up for a career change. Or you decide you want to become a chef and going to culinary school seems like the next logical step.

This boils down to whether the degree will ultimately put you in a better place than if you had worked for that one or two-year period instead. Crunch the numbers, do the deep thinking. Here are some details to consider:

- Does your organization pretty much require an advanced degree or MBA for all senior positions? Some companies do, some don't. Some dislike applicants with MBAs in favor of those with more on-the-job experience.
- Will your current organization teach you the skills you want learn?
- Do you want to stay in the current industry / role, or move to a new one? Employers want either real experience or specialized education from an applicant suitable for a position, and if you plan a hard shift in a new direction, school may be the best option.
- What are the possibilities and benefits in staying where you are in terms of promotions and compensation increases?
- Will the type of position and remuneration you can get with an MBA or advanced degree be that much better than having worked during that period?

Making a Decision

Mull over the answers to all of the questions and options about career changes carefully. One helpful tool is to use a single piece of paper and write down the pros of your current position on the left side and the cons on the right side. Flip the paper over, and make three columns on this side. In the left column, write down your current compensation and your current responsibilities. In the middle column, write down your "ideal" compensation and responsibilities for your next career stage. (Don't be overly cautious here, but be realistic. Use tools like salary websites to establish some norms.) For the right column, write down the career opportunities out there that you are finding. How do they stack up? Are there any opportunities better than your current position, let alone that stack up against your ideal position? Throw in school if that is a consideration.

Make some unrushed, well-balanced assessments and you will find the right direction. Don't stress out over the idea that every single career choice you ever make has to be perfect. Almost everyone has periods that aren't ideal. It is more important that you don't stay in a less-than-ideal place, but pivot and continue forward.

Chapter 19: Leaving an Organization

Money. Family. Happiness. Opportunity. Stress (or lack of). Countless reasons abound as to why you might be planning to leave your organization. People leave organizations, it is a fact of life. Once you make that decision, it is of more concern to plan how you handle that change and optimize the outcome, not only for yourself, but your co-workers, boss and organization.

If at all possible, do not to leave with just two weeks' notice. (Or less!) There aren't many circumstances that keep you from knowing well in advance that you won't be in your position much longer. Sudden family or health circumstances are an exception, but in most other cases, you know many weeks or even months in advance, particularly if you are a planner.

Here is the main argument that people provide for giving only two weeks' notice. "My company would let me go as soon as they found someone else and I need to be working for that period of time to make money (or any other reason)." Unfortunately, if you are fairly certain that your boss or organization wouldn't honor your notice and would decide to fire you immediately, then give just the two weeks. It's a judgement call on your part, but do your research and find out what the process has been like for others in a similar situation previously. Any other co-worker that has been in the organization a long period of time will likely know.

Fears of immediate termination aside, here's why you should try to give as much notice as reasonably possible:

- **You don't stick your peers in a tough situation.** Especially if you work in a close-knit team, your co-workers get the short end of the stick, scrambling to do all of the things they thought you would be doing if you hadn't given short notice. It is a poor situation in which to leave people.

- **You maintain professional connections and a network.** A strong network will be very important throughout your career. Cutting ties when you leave vaporizes that; it is one of those lessons you don't want to learn the hard way.
- **You avoid damaging future career prospects.** References and past employers get called by potential employers. If you do give at least two weeks' notice, most employers won't fault you very much. But not all people are kind or logical. Some employers will dislike you for a sudden departure and will give either neutral or poor references of character or performance. That's very different from a grateful employer who says, "Jane let us know six weeks before she left, and worked very hard to make the transition as seamless as possible."
- **You don't stick your boss or the organization in a tough situation.** If they have been good to you, it shows a lack of consideration or respect to quit suddenly.

What is your position in the organization? Do your co-workers have overlapping responsibilities that allows the organization to at least stop-gap the loss from your departure? Or do you have a unique role in the organization or have a harder-to-find skillset that requires a lot of hunting for suitable candidates?

If you get the answers to the above and you feel your boss / organization will (as they should) respond pragmatically and work with you on the transition, that is the best possible route.

Streamline your departure and minimize negatives by:

- **Giving as much notice as you think is possible.** Unless you think it will result in you being fired.
- **Preparing for the transition.** Someone or multiple people will have to take over your workload. Leave documentation and advice for those who will follow you.
- **Helping to fill the position.** Either helping to search for other candidates, and / or assisting in the interview and evaluation process.
- **Getting references / recommendations.** Whether you are applying for another position or going back to school, a

supervisor's recommendation counts for a lot. In your last days, ask them to write a recommendation while you are still fresh in their mind.

- **Being available for questions after you leave.** Don't work long hours for free for your previous employer. But you can let them and your replacement(s) know that for a month or six weeks, you can be reached by email to answer any questions and that you will respond as soon as you can.

Be understanding of the hole your departure creates and the benefits you receive by easing the transition as much as possible.

Section Seven: Leadership

You may never want to become a formal manager responsible for things like payroll, hiring / firing, or larger strategic decisions. But between being a strong individual contributor and a formal manager, there are many needs and opportunities for leadership.

Chapter 20: Project Management

Some areas in an organization are your own; daily responsibilities, smaller tasks, you take care of these items with your own efforts.

Then you have larger initiatives that involve more than yourself, such as working with other people and / or coordinating tools, materials, and other resources toward a specific set of goals. These are projects. Each project's success depends on more than one person, yet at the same time, it benefits greatly from a chief organizer.

Sometimes your supervisor will act in that capacity, and other times he or she will assign someone from the team to take the lead. If you are not the official project manager, you can still take up responsibilities more informally to help arrive at a good conclusion. When you don't have an official mandate, peer management, the subject of the next chapter, becomes vital. Well thought-out projects have good plans and effective leadership. That is easy to say, but how do you do it?

Planning the Project

Start planning as follows:

1) Discuss the desired outcome with all stakeholders. The end return of the project and / or the deadline by which it should be completed.

2) Research the required resources: internal and external, people, money, and materials required to get the job done.

3) Assemble the project plan (covered below) and project budget (covered in Chapter 16).

4) Review and agree upon the project plan and budget with stakeholders based upon your assessments of time and resource requirements.

5) Ensure that everyone has a clear sense of the goal(s) of the project and expectations on them.

6) Assign out all responsibilities.

7) Go!

As far as planning the project, it really comes down to figuring out who has to do what, when, and with which resources. As fancy or simple as you like, document the various assignments and responsibilities of each person or team and what resources they will need to use or procure to do their portion. Gantt charts are a favored tool for project planning because they help people visualize how the different timelines of a project overlap, and in what order they must be done.

Have every discrete requirement of the project documented out, something done either by yourself or better yet, by the person(s) assigned to that particular element. These are the commitments to which you can hold each person or resource accountable.

A few additional tips:

- **Avoid over-planning.** It is one thing to assess all of the variables to create a thorough project plan and another to try and account for every possible variable, or get 100% of people to agree on the tiniest of details. Problems most often occur when there are too many people involved in decisions, when there is not a clear leader who makes the final decisions, or both.

- **Create multiple planning periods, instead of simply one at the beginning**. The planning phase of a project must be worked on first, but don't try to get every last element finalized before you begin. There are always wildcards in projects. When you lose the fluidity to adapt to circumstances because you are locked into a project plan, you create a less-than-optimal result, which actually results in more time and resources wasted, first from the original plan and then pivoting to an entirely new one.

- **Overlap planning and execution.** With multiple planning periods, begin what work you can as soon as you can do it. In a project, some elements will be required or necessary and are not subject to change later. Or they utilize resources you already have versus resources you need to acquire. Start on those items as soon as possible.

- **Give yourself padding with time and resources.** Even the most well-aligned teams that have done many projects together have unexpected issues come up. With any area of the project where you are less than 95% sure you can deliver within the time and resource parameters, give yourself a bit of cushion. Don't go too far with the cushion. Coming in a bit below budget or before the time will be embraced by all, but organizations want fairly accurate estimates they can plan by.

Managing the Project

For a dependable, nimble method of project management, follow these steps:

1) Establish regular check-ins with each person / team / functional area.

2) Hold regular supplemental planning sessions to address new details that come up and to ensure that the original project plan still applies or is still the best approach.

3) Ensure that everyone has the required resources to complete their portion.

4) Hold each person (or team, or vendor) accountable to their commitments.

5) Report up to the principal stakeholders to keep them apprised of status of the project and any changes in time or required resources.

6) Get the project completed and relax (for at least a bit). You've done well.

Your goal is to figure out whatever it takes to get the project done. That can mean making hard decisions. If someone isn't able to handle their part, you will end up either needing to help them, locating an additional resource (another person or people) to help them, or making the decision to replace them with another who can do the task. If you are the official manager, that can be easy, if not, it requires frank conversations with that person, team, or your own boss.

A few additional thoughts:

- **Keep everyone focused on the end-goal and bigger picture.** Don't make the project about individual goals or egos. The desired outcome is what matters; everyone should be working together toward that end.
- **Step back and assess regularly.** As a project manager, you are involved in the details so much that you can lose the broader perspective. Make sure to step back and study where things are going well and where they are not; where the project seems to be evolving well, and where new factors (or factors you didn't previously consider) will mandate modifications.
- **Verify, but don't be a chokepoint.** If you have an actual need to be part of every discrete step or task of the larger project, fine, but otherwise trust others to do a good job. You still assist by checking in regularly and providing additional input and resources, but you can't scale in large ways if everything must go through you for approval.
- **Project delays.** With regular check-ins, you shouldn't have many "large" surprises, but regardless of their size, whenever something occurs that will impact the agreed-upon outcome, relay that immediately to stakeholders.
- **Manage expectations.** The best approach is a balanced one. Don't get stakeholders too excited by hyping up one smaller success only to have to share bad news the next time. The real high point for everyone should come when the project has concluded.

Project management has its difficulties, but so do smaller tasks. It feel good to be part of something larger, more so when you successfully accomplish it.

Chapter 21: Peer Management

"Managing peers" sounds like an oxymoron at first. If someone is your peer or co-worker and you aren't formally managing him or her, is it really management?

A formal supervisor or manager doesn't necessarily have to be a great, or even good, leader. But when they tell one of their reports to do something, that person is expected to carry out the task. They don't have much choice in the matter if their supervisor insists that a (reasonable / ethical) task be completed in a certain manner by a certain date. There is a wide gulf between having formal management power and being able to apply it effectively. (The subject of Part Two).

Assigning one person in a team to be the de facto project manager for a special project is a middle ground. The supervisor can tell the entire team that while the project manager isn't their actual supervisor, he or she is responsible for the project's completion. That makes the project manager's job somewhat easier, but is still not the same as being the official manager.

Projects aside, the reality is that teams of people who are in peer / co-worker relationships must regularly execute tasks together. High-level details may be provided by the official manager, but the tactics, the day-to-day execution, relies on those peers working together. Not only does this occur in groups under the same manager, but also frequently between people that report to different managers. How does a person who isn't an actual manager, effectively work with others to affect the best possible results?

They do it by peer management. Peer management is the art of working with your peers. A peer manager isn't a supervisor. They can't really tell their co-worker what to do. They must rely on their own work and reputation, empathy, logic, and communication skills to get everyone else to work with them.

Peer management is critical for two reasons:

1) The ability to harness others' potential in addition to your own is how you create the largest successes.
2) If you can't manage your peers well before you become a formal manager, you won't lead them very well and maximize your team's potential when or if you do rise to that role.

Everyone knows a good peer manager within his or her organization. It's that person who doesn't have formal seniority over his or her peers, but is viewed by everyone as the second in command behind the actual supervisor.

It isn't a popularity contest. Peer management requires the ability to help make the tough decisions and change people's perspectives (which can take quite a lot of convincing), but it is the approach and ability to enact that change, without requiring the supervisor's constant involvement, that makes the difference.

A Change in Thinking

Up until you graduate from school, you are judged and graded primarily on your individual performance. You compete with your peers for the best grades, for the top slots. After graduation, some of that certainly remains, such as applying for job positions and completing any tasks assigned only to you. But the fact is that you have been trained much of your life to compete against other individuals.

Organizations, however, are composed of more than one person. The man or woman who can harness the talent and resources of his or her team will end up achieving much more than the person who fights everyone but themselves. This is one reason that team sports players do so well in many types of professional careers; in those sports, it is the combined efforts of all that lead to victory.

Pillars of Peer Management

To be a successful peer manager takes:

- Being good at your skills and stated strengths.
- Knowing your weaknesses and being open about them
- Developing a reputation based on supporting others.
- Using your communication skills and empathy to understand perspectives.
- Creating shared perspectives that align people with you.
- Recognizing and utilizing others' skills and contributions.
- Acknowledging the value of others and their contributions.
- Being calm when unexpected situations occur.

Remember that you are not the formal manager, so it is about guiding, not pushing. You are building equity with others by giving more than you get most of the time. When you are asked to help with something, smile and help. (Remember, "How can I help you?") Of course, you can't sacrifice your own work to help someone else and you don't want people simply pushing excess work on you. Help others where you can on basic work but really try to be a resource for larger-scale initiatives or planning sessions that have greater implications for the team and the organization.

Instead of always arguing your own points, develop the mindset of arguing other's points as much as your own. It isn't about compromises, but realizing that you aren't the only smart one in the organization. If your points are valid, go with them, but listen to others first. Create a sense of cooperation and shared priorities. Whenever you cannot make a conclusive decision as to whether one path is right or wrong, figure out if there is a way to test both on a limited scale. Instead of ego and argument, allow the results to speak and move on.

At the end of the day, peer management is incredibly satisfying. Learning to harness the power of multiple people's efforts to achieve big things is the type of challenge and reward that makes a career enjoyable.

Conclusion

If you apply all of the methods and outlooks presented in Part One in the course of your career, ahead of or better than your peers, you are going to succeed big. When your peers like you, and your boss looks to you to get things done, you will have many opportunities come your way.

Part Two: Becoming a Successful Manager

Section One: Preparing for Management

A formal management position is not required to succeed big professionally. You can be a specialist in your particular field, and fulfill all of your professional, financial, and personal ambitions without ever being a formal supervisor. However, projects and endeavors after a certain size require strategy and organization. Perhaps you wish to be a manager, perhaps not, but if you are to become one, there is a right way and wrong way to do it.

There are many bad managers out there. It is also an unfortunate truth that many good, even stellar, contributors (employees, workers, or volunteers) make only adequate managers, or worse. Most men and women are simply thrown into management positions with no preparation or direction. Some fly, some sink.

What is it that makes the difference between a good manager and a poor one? Between a great contributor and a poor manager? Part Two goes into detail on two core principles: strategy development and building quality teams of people. Grasp these two concepts, implement them, and you will have no limits.

Chapter 22: What It Means to be a Manager

Every person in an organization - be it a Fortune 500 company, a start-up, a non-profit, or the military - falls somewhere on the contributor-manager spectrum:

As you move left to right on the spectrum, the blend of doing the work, versus managing it, shifts. The men and women on the far left part of the spectrum are the ones with no official management responsibilities. They carry out tasks that need to be done.

As you gain experience and do that work well, you may receive more responsibilities and promotions to your first formal management duties - much like a corporal or sergeant - leading a team (moving to the right on the spectrum). A great sergeant parallels a great team leader; a person who is the first among peers. He or she has the experience from having recently been a more junior soldier. That experience translates into tactical insight and knowing all of the tips and tricks of the job. He or she is the example to which everyone else on the team aspires. The sergeant not only influences the strategies in the unit and develops the team, he or she is also in the middle of the fight. Similarly, a team leader teaches and imparts his or her knowledge upon their subordinates (managing) while still playing a more hands-on role in controlling how various elements come together and making sophisticated tweaks (doing).

The far-right end of the spectrum is the domain of senior managers and executives in the organization. They don't carry out the tasks themselves; they make decisions on the best way(s) to carry out those tasks (strategy) and leading others to do so (management).

While a general in the military may once have been a great marksmen, or set records in endurance, those days are long gone. But the general has a wealth of experience in an area where the more junior officers don't: the shaping of strategy and the marshalling of resources (people, materials, and funds). It is the ability to do those two things well that gives the general a lofty position.

While there are many differences between a team leader and a CEO (or a sergeant and a general, respectively), the success of these individuals relies on effectively doing two critical things:

1) Crafting Strategy
2) Building Talent & Teams

The only difference between the team leader and the CEO is that the (good) CEO has been doing these two things for a long time and has the benefit of experience, while a team leader begins with no direct experience to draw on. *The entire separation between the two positions is a function only of the ability of a manager to successfully manage strategies and build the talent in their organization.*

Set aside age, gender, race, education, culture, background. Around the world, in any organization, it is the fruitful application - or not - of these two skills that creates excellence.

For some talented individuals, these skills come more naturally or they build these skills earlier in life through analogous experiences (such as sports). Great entrepreneurs often naturally possess a good measure of both of these skills. For everyone else, an awareness of the importance of these skills, and their actual implementation makes the difference.

You can be an amazing worker, but until you realize you can't do everything yourself, you will only limit your ultimate ability to create growth, for yourself or for your organization. Managers of small to mid-sized teams most often make this mistake, and it is one that can limit them from ever going further. These managers are bottlenecks, as everything must go through them and they therefore end up focusing more on the smallest of details than any strategic decision making.

This occurs with more senior professionals as well. Size only makes the end outcome worse. Take for example a company of 200 people. An executive - Director / Vice-President / CEO - might have three or four trusted lieutenants established over the years that ensure the required work gets done, but that executive is still the one doing all of the crisis-solving and, in focusing on that, he or she loses sight of broader decision making, which ends up being done well by no one. The team experiences no growth or development because it relies on one person, instead of that one person being a guiding light for growth in new initiatives and growth in people.

Your ability to shape strategy with the resources you are given, and grow those resources – which in turn allows you to further craft your strategy – will dictate a large extent of your success in organizations as a manager. The entirety of Part Two of this book deals with the best ways of approaching strategy and building teams.

Chapter 23: Types of Management

There are many styles of management that people employ, stemming from their background, personality, education, and leadership experience. Most men and women never receive formal management training. A few are natural leaders; others gain skills through sports, school clubs, early jobs, or military service. All of this informs a leadership approach. Some leaders are extroverts, some introverts. Some like to be very friendly with the men and women under their command, others always maintain a strong line, not sharing anything personal. Some build teams through steady coaching and supervision, while others believe hard lessons in experience are more effective. The list goes on and on.

The extremes of any one management style will cause headaches and frustrations, but within those limits, there isn't any one "right" answer. Beyond individual background, the culture of the organization and the particular industry or area also impact the applied style of management. None, however, change the need to focus on crafting strategy and building teams.

The truer - and more universal - assessment of management efficacy lies in assessing whether you are an active or reactive manager.

Active vs. Reactive Management

One of the pivotal themes in the Part One of this book pertains to actively seeking out opportunities to help your team or your organization as a way of elevating your career path. That isn't always easy when you are very busy with work or goals that have already been assigned to you. Yet the men and women who not only complete their own tasks, but also pay attention to and assist with the larger needs of the team are the ones who create advancement opportunities for themselves.

Reactive managers operate in a perpetual crisis mode, responding to problems that emerge within their teams or in their strategy (getting to their goals), and to the new goals they receive from their bosses, customers, and vendors. They move from one situation to another, fixing issues as quickly as possible. There is more of a focus on removing the issue in the immediate term with a quick "patch" instead of investing more time in putting processes and solutions in place to keep those problems from happening over and over. One month to another yields little change in developing new solutions or increasing forward momentum. Strategy development suffers and little team growth occurs.

Every manager in the world performs some of this reactive type of approach (it is almost impossible not to), especially in already-busy times when something unexpected comes along. However, reactive managers work in this fashion the majority of the time, creating a static atmosphere.

Active managers do things a little differently in the beginning to generate very different results in the end. Whenever a new or unexpected issue comes up, the active manager thinks not only about the immediate solution, but also whether the issue is going to occur again or is occurring in other areas of the organization. In cases where the issue may crop up again, the active manager invests a bit more time in developing a solution that reduces the impact or frequency, or both.

He or she anticipates problems based on experience and thinking ahead about possible outcomes. For instance they might think, "It is likely that the new team lead I put into place is going to struggle developing the sales strategy in this new market. I struggled initially and the other people I have assigned to that role struggled initially as well. I should develop a framework that helps the team lead understand the dynamics, ensure that the team lead speaks with me and other people who have been in that position, and that I organize a 15-minute meeting weekly for the next few months to keep aware of the situation and support the new person."

The active manager sets aside time to think about short and long-term strategy, and how to pivot that based on new developments. If that manager finds out that the team is going to get a customer that is ten times the size of previous customers, he or she will think about potential issues and bottlenecks ahead of time, and proactively engage this large customer as quickly as possible to identify where new problems might emerge. That is very different from simply reacting after the fact. Sure, there are going to be problems that weren't anticipated, but the more that can be anticipated and structured, the better the end result will be. As another example, if that manager works in an industry wherein each new client is a fairly unique case, which means there are almost always a few days of troubleshooting and tweaking, the active manager will plan for that troubleshooting time in the team or organization's schedule.

Last, but not least, the active manager scales his or her ability to contribute by hiring and nurturing talented people that help him or her achieve all of the aforementioned items. The active manager then becomes freer to focus on the few crises that truly require his or her involvement, new strategy, and mentoring more talented contributors for the organization. It is a positive cycle of growth.

Every great manager uses this active framework, irrespective of leadership style or influence. Within that framework, you can develop your own unique tactics and approaches to management that suit your personality and your needs, but it all revolves around strategic thinking and effective teams of people.

Chapter 24: Management Training

When great contributors fail in their first formal managerial roles, the persons to blame most are their supervisors. The vast majority of managers in organizations receive little to no preparation for the skillsets of thinking strategically and building teams. They are chosen based on personal performance and suddenly thrust into these new roles, with a sink or swim attitude.

While the largest organizations in the world have management training programs, most lack such a formal structure. Lessons come either the easy way - through observation and coaching by a supervisor or mentor prior to assuming such responsibilities - or the hard way - through learning the lessons and making the mistakes on the spot. Not all lessons will be learned the easy way, but many of the hard lessons can be taught beforehand.

One of the critical things to do as soon as you decide to pursue a management track is to evaluate whether your current organization (or one you are applying to) thinks about management in the right way and develops managerial skillsets in its people. Items to figure out:

- Is there a formal management development track in the organization? Some may be complete programs; other organizations may assign senior managers to coach new or aspiring managers.
- Does your (current or future) supervisor have a history of helping people develop into managers, have no history, or do they have a poor history?
- What are the key elements that the organization emphasizes in its managers?

- Are decisions made on data presented or are they made arbitrarily based on biases, moods, or incomplete information?

You can certainly apply to and revolutionize an organization that has poor managers, but you first need to have the opportunity to learn management skills in a supportive environment. That environment could be a business school program or it could be in an industry or organization that isn't a long-term fit, but a wonderful shorter-term place to grow.

Once you have the right environment, take these steps:

- Identify great managers and mentors.
- Observe how your boss (if you respect him or her and their management style) and other managers perform their roles.
- Learn from mentors. Learn from books.
- Ask many questions. Especially questions of your supervisor and manager about the hows and whys of decisions made around strategy and building teams.
- Implement and test lessons learned in your own day-to-day tasks and routines.
- Volunteer for activities and projects that require and grow skills in crafting strategy and building teams.

Gaining Experience

It is worth expanding on the point of implementing and testing management concepts before you are formal manager. Peer management (covered in Part One) teaches you a base amount of skills to go into your first management positions. Don't stop there though. You don't have to wait to gain experience in an area until you are assigned that duty. Furthermore, not all experiences are created equal.

Most forms of martial arts use a ranking system to distinguish a beginner - a "white belt" - from successively more experienced practitioners, such as an "orange belt" or a "blue belt." The more senior practitioners have passed the tests to receive their higher ranks, but what truly separates them? Experience. In martial arts, this comes down to quantity and quality of practice. The average "white belt" with a month of experience may have practiced a particular kick 500 times. An average "orange belt" with six months of experience will have practiced that same kick 3000 times. The act of having performed that same kick so many more times makes the difference.

But does that mean that the "white belt" must wait another five months to gain the same proficiency? Never. That "white belt" can practice his or her kick many more times than average and gain experience that way, or he or she can pay more attention to studying and developing the quality the kick (the technique). If that "white belt" continues in this fashion, he or she will surpass first peers, and soon, seniors who have been there far longer.

Going back to the professional world, don't think of experience as a time-based, linear concept. Gain experience more quickly by:

- Enacting management concepts as much as possible in your day-to-day activities and other venues (such as hobbies, sports, and volunteer opportunities).
- Breaking down complex management tasks into smaller areas you can understand and enact.
- Planning and executing every decision with care and deliberation.
- Analyzing the results afterward (positive and negative) to learn from them.

The more times you can practice something (in part or in its entirety) the more familiar you will become with it. That is an obvious statement, but not one that many apply in the professional world until directed to do so. Don't rely on others to always hand you opportunities, make your own. Sit in on strategy meetings. Participate in hiring processes (reviewing resumes with a supervisor, conducting peer interviews, etc.). Figure out what your supervisor does that you don't yet know how to do and learn it.

Practice as many times as possible and make those practice runs as high-quality and as educational as you can. It comes back to the theme of learning to do things before you are expected to do them. If you wish to become a senior manager in an organization, you have to demonstrate skillsets on par with other candidates for the position, and that requires experience. If you can showcase such skills to a current or potential supervisor, you will receive opportunities to advance.

Proactive learning of these skills will ensure that by the time you become a manager, you will start with a greater depth of experience and expertise compared to other new managers.

Section Two: Assuming Leadership

The day has come: your first formal leadership position. Where to start? Before you take actions, large or small, you need to understand what has happened in the past and what is going on now, in the team's strategy, the organization's strategy, and within the team itself. The following chapters address evaluating strategy and evaluating your team.

If your management role will be in an organization you currently work for (the product of a promotion), you start with what can either be a positive or a negative: your knowledge of the organization. On the positive side, you likely know a lot about the team's current objectives and strategies. You also often have time to make assessments and create a plan before your next position officially begins. On the negative side, your insider's perspective might make you blind to bigger issues that you don't see because you view them as acceptable or have never learned another way of doing things.

Whether new or old to the organization, take the time to figure out what is going on and why. Some newer managers adopt a "slash and burn" approach in their first weeks on a job, making a large number of changes in personnel and strategy quickly. Unfortunately, this often results in letting good people go with the bad and the repetition of strategies and actions that have been tried before with no success.

When you do come across an issue, don't make quick judgments before you have all of the information. You are more likely to make a poor decision when you don't have the full picture; and if you create new processes based on that incomplete picture, you are going to create more damage within your team, with clients, or across the entire organization. Good assessment goes hand-in-hand with working collaboratively with the major stakeholders. As the saying goes, "measure twice, cut once." Ideas are a dime a dozen; it is the proper execution of even average ideas - with the right plan and good people - that makes the difference.

Chapter 25: Evaluating Your Strategy

Your first job as a manager, whether you have one person reporting to you or one thousand, is to understand the objectives of your team and direct (create and / or update) the strategy of that team to meet those objectives. You can't know what people or resources you will require to execute those objectives unless you understand the strategy. If the strategy currently employed isn't going to get you to your assigned objectives, you need to figure that out as soon as possible up front, versus waiting and coming across unexpected surprises and setbacks.

Research What Is Going On

The following questions are useful in evaluating the current strategy:

- What are the objectives of the team and why are they important?
- How do the objectives roll up into the larger organizational strategy?
- Does the strategy at least fulfill - and hopefully exceed - the needs of the key constituent?
- Why was the strategy created?
- Who created the strategy? Are they still around to consult?
- How is the strategy supposed to work?
- Has the current strategy worked before (to achieve the objectives) in your team, other teams, or other organizations?
- Have other strategies been attempted historically to reach those objectives? How successful or unsuccessful were they and why were they abandoned?

- How well is the strategy working right now? Are the objectives being met (by a large or small margin) or are they being missed?
- If the strategy is failing to meet objectives, what can you (and / or others) specifically attribute the failures to?
- What are the resources (people and otherwise) required to fulfill the strategy?

Talk to everyone you can, inside and outside of your team, and outside of your organization as well, to gain a full picture of the current and past status of the strategy. Everyone will have their own viewpoint about the historical failures and successes, or suggestions on changes they believe will bring in better results. You can end up disagreeing with every person you've spoken to and dismiss the entire strategy currently in place, but you have at least gained valuable perspective to know what else has been tried in the past. Don't reinvent the wheel.

What if there is no real strategy in place? This happens quite frequently, especially in cases where an organization moves into brand new objectives or decides to build a new team with you at its helm. In those cases, you will be creating a strategy from the ground up.

Stabilize & Prime the Strategy

Your priority in the first days in your management role is to meet immediate needs and stabilize the current trajectory of the team. Each industry and profession will dictate their own specific needs, but there are a few nearly universal categories:

- Crises and situations that demand and draw negative attention to you, your team, or your organization, both recurring as well as one-time events.
- Operational (tactical) decisions and actions that are hurting or hindering the execution of the strategy.
- Small changes that can lead to large or quick results. This sometimes depends on having had direct experience in a particular role or scenario before.
- Missing or incomplete resources to properly enact the strategy.

Even if you are developing a strategy from scratch, there are always going to be certain foundational elements on which you can begin working on to build initial momentum.

In the case of larger strategic changes, you have to factor in the time to not only create the initial plan, but also manage expectations of changes with all involved parties, including those on your team, your supervisors, your customers, and your partners.

Create Your Improvement Plan(s)

Crafting a long-term plan requires the above-mentioned research coupled with your experience and original thinking. (A later section in the book discusses strategy development in detail.) This is the strategic plan meant to drive sustained or bettered achievement of the team's objectives. If you know the scenario well enough or have the time, you may be able to create the longer-term strategic plan in a few weeks, but you won't have it done right away.

In addressing immediate needs and getting your bearings, create a short-term action plan before committing to a longer one (if possible). Your short-term plan may be anywhere from one to four weeks (Day 1 to Day 30). It allows you some breathing room to really research and dig into how the team and organization functions day-to-day in achieving its objectives.

The short-term improvement plan should also allow you enough latitude to begin the second part of the evaluation process, reviewing the people on your team.

Chapter 26: Evaluating Your Team

As soon as (or at the same time as) you resolve any existing crises, you must evaluate your team. Regardless of the size of your team or number of people reporting to you, you need to establish the role and quality of those people.

The initial evaluation process follows much of the track that you might use to interview candidates for a new job, but it is easier insofar as you typically have more tangible data and proof of a person's contributions and quality of work. You want to be as thorough as you can be in evaluating a team member. These evaluations and their following actions are best done immediately when you start your new position and / or 30 days after you have worked with that person.

Your ability to make judgments immediately about someone's potential depends greatly on your experience and track record of hiring. If you have neither, give that person 30 days to show you what they can do instead of making an arbitrary decision based on limited information.

Initial Evaluations

Read through each team member's resume and personnel file. Personnel files vary wildly between organizations; some are valuable, some are not. The unfortunate truth is that many personnel files have very little content: a person's resume, annual reviews, and any incident reports that may have occurred, as opposed to detailed write-ups by prior managers of that person's skills, strengths, and weaknesses. This means you are likely starting from close to scratch in your evaluation process.

Sit down individually with each person on the team. Speak with them, their peers, and supervisors (current and former) to figure out the following:

- What each person specifically contributes toward the strategy.
- Can they explain their day-to-day responsibilities well or do you get the sense they don't accomplish very much?
- Is there a history or track record of meeting expectations or missing them?
- What do peers say about a particular person?
- What does the former supervisor say about a given individual?
- [For managers on your team] What do the manager's direct reports say (or not say) about him or her?

If you are coming into a management role with a layer of managers below you, speak not only to those managers (your direct or "first-level" reports), but also to their direct reports (your "second-level" reports). You can of course go more than two levels deep, but most of the effective change will come from assessing those two layers.

Many of these questions may feel like an interview process, and they should, because to your new team, that is exactly what they are. (Never call these first meetings "interviews"...) They will be just as - or more - nervous in speaking to a new boss as they would be interviewing for a new position. Most will know little or nothing about you, and therefore have no idea about whether you are fair and balanced or random in your decision-making; they will also not know whether you have already decided to remove certain people from the team. Assume that your first conversations with a person won't portray the whole of his or her true nature - good or bad.

Any opinions you get from a single third party about another person should be discounted unless or until you completely trust that person's opinion. You likely don't yet know any of the personal history or office politics that may be driving any one person's viewpoint, but in greater numbers, opinions do become more relevant. Look for patterns in what multiple people say about a particular person, as well as your own observations. If enough people say there is smoke, there is usually a fire.

The first round of meetings with your new team will produce two important results:

- Identification of the obvious poor contributors on the team.
- A baseline and expectations for each person from which you can benchmark the following 30+ days of their actions and performance.

Just like hiring interviews (covered in later chapters in detail), if you don't know enough about a particular person's role or expertise to make an informed decision, it is advisable to bring in an expert or someone you do trust to help you make the initial assessment. For the areas in which you have the background, it is easier to quickly tell how someone's performance stacks up in their history and in the way they discuss their contributions with you.

With the obvious poor contributors, it is your decision as to whether you believe you can train and mold them into better contributors, or if you feel they have little upside growth opportunity. It depends in part on how entrenched they seem in their current methods and views versus being more open to continued learning and expansion.

Ongoing Evaluations & Plans

The team's strategic plan dictates the types of people and skillsets required. Therefore, you should think not only about whether each person is good or bad in absolute terms, but also how relevant each person's skills and expertise are in executing the strategy. That aspect, in and of itself, is a good argument to not rush to make personnel changes in a team. Anyone who seems poisonous or lacks the ability to change in a positive way is one thing, but if you are still working on developing or cleaning up the team's strategy, waiting for a short period is the better option. The person that currently performs a role that seems irrelevant to you might pivot very well into a more important role once you clarify the new strategy and expectations.

As you gain a feel for the dynamic of the team and its culture, you will also begin to recognize:

- The leaders in the team.
- The people who seemed initially great, but who simply gave a good first impression, based on their subsequent performance and your observations.

- Who doesn't seem to contribute much to the team's strategy, and why. Is it poorly defined expectations, poor execution on their part, or poor management?

If you believe that most managers are average, you will regularly come into situations where there is much to be gained by introducing a great manager. You will need to learn to separate poor performance that can be tied back to that individual, versus poor performance because of the direction and management (or lack of) by a former supervisor.

Ensure that you paint as clear a picture as possible to every person on the team in explaining your core philosophies and strategic plans; if you don't have them compiled yet, be transparent. People desire good direction. Set well-defined expectations with every person on an individual level, as well as the expectations for the team's overall performance.

30-day (or other short-term) plans are helpful in setting expectations. Even if you are still working on the broader strategy, you may feel shorter term changes and pivots to be important to improving results or simply setting the foundation for larger changes later on.

By the time you have concluded your first sets of meetings with your team, you should have achieved the principal goals of learning the current state (or lack) of a strong strategy, gained an initial sense of who exactly makes up your team, and the potential talent you have in it. This gives you the foundation to start making more far-reaching strategic decisions and building a strong team.

Section Three: Strategy Development

Strategy: The big decisions and guidelines that steer a team or an organization. People look at successful organizations and say, "that organization has an amazing strategy, they predicted the market." What does that mean though? Did the organization's leaders see into the future and forecast what would happen? Did they develop the strategy in a day? Do all of the multi-billion dollar organizations out there operate exactly as when they first started? The answer to all of these is "no." Warren Buffett, the billionaire investor, certainly seems to be a seer. Mark Zuckerberg, the founder of Facebook, started something that has impacted the very way people interact with one another. But even these amazingly successful people didn't come up with a perfect model on day one.

Success doesn't materialize instantaneously or magically. Even Warren Buffet and Mark Zuckerberg have a string of failures among their successes. It was and is their ability to study, analyze, and adapt to new opportunities, over and over, that has vaulted them to their respective levels.

There is no such thing as a perfect strategy. But there is a good strategy for every opportunity and there are many opportunities out there.

Chapter 27: Understanding Strategy

Do you know your organization's key mission or reason for existence? Good strategies are clearly established plans and guidelines that support and deliver on the mission of the organization.

Strategies exist:

- At the industry level
- At the organization's level
- At the division / department level
- At the team level
- In every major product or channel

Entire industries have a generally similar strategy of why they exist and how they appeal to their customers, clients, or donors. Organizations within those industries adopt a variant of that strategy to carve out their own space for success. Within an organization, divisions and departments produce strategies that each fulfill a part of the organization's mission. Teams create strategies that achieve the goals of the division and the overall organization.

At every level, there exists an opportunity to develop and iterate on the strategy. The greater the amount of resources involved, the slower these changes typically occur. That is why start-up companies, much more nimble than their larger competitors, are often the ones to transform an industry by changing the old way of doing things and introducing the new way.

The question to always ask is whether the strategy of a

particular division or team within an organization supports the organization's overall strategy and mission, or not. Many smaller strategies actually don't sync with the larger strategies and cause friction or limit growth versus propelling it.

Strategy vs. Tactics

It is vital to distinguish between strategy and tactics. Strategy is the "big picture" guiding the mission of the team. It goes hand-in-hand with the mission of the broader organization.

Here's an example of a clear strategy: Imaginary Pet Products is a fictional company, whose mission it is to be the premier manufacturer and distributor of natural, additive-free pet food for cats. The strategy of Imaginary Pet Products revolves around two elements: 1) to set up manufacturing plants in areas next to large supplies of the ingredients that go into their pet food, in order to achieve low costs and transportation efficiency, and 2) strong marketing campaigns to the public that build the brand. Imaginary Pet Products knows that if it can execute on these two elements well, the odds of success are in its favor. Every major decision that the company makes must revolve around those two areas to keep the company focused.

This strategy may work very well for the company, but to be successful over the long-term, strategy must be fluid and evolve over time based on changes in its customers, vendors, employees, or broader macro-economic factors. For instance, three years from now, Imaginary Pet Products may have done a great job executing on its two-prong strategy and decides to expand its mission to be the premier provider of natural pet food to all domestic animals, including dogs, birds, etc.

When a team's strategy properly aligns with the organization's strategy, great things happen. When there is a misalignment, many resources are wasted. Going back to the Imaginary Pet Products example, if the procurement team of the company – which focuses on getting the best possible cost efficiencies – strikes a deal to buy the pet food bags at 90% of the cost of the prior bags, that might be wonderful. However, if getting those bags at 90% means that the quality of those bags deteriorates and removes the ability to print high-end graphics on them, that may be a great mistake if it prevents the marketing department from showcasing a premier brand and leads consumers to view the quality of the product as declining. The point here is that the procurement team must consider its team's strategy in the context of the broader organization. Are the things they are doing complementary? That may simply mean having the meetings and conversations with the managers in the organization to study the pros and cons of the decision(s).

As another example: a nursing home for seniors has a mission to be the premier luxury provider of care in The United States. The strategy driving that mission focuses on 1) building and maintaining high-end apartments that appeal to this higher-end market, and 2) excellent food for residents, which separate it from the competition. Let's say that the marketing of the nursing home occupies 20% of the time of the two senior operations people and the quality of the marketing campaigns is very average, as they don't have the expertise in-house. Strategically it may make sense to outsource the marketing to an agency that has a specialty in geriatric services marketing. The nursing home wins first by putting out much higher-end marketing and, second, by allowing its operations people to focus the core elements of the strategy: the apartment quality and the food services. These are the types of strategic decisions that separate the nursing home from competitors and allow it have a keen operational focus.

Every department, every team, and every individual in the organization should follow the strategy if it is clearly defined. (Again, to stress the fact, strategy does change over time and the contribution of even a single person can reshape the entire organization's strategy because of new information or a new perspective.)

Below the level of the overall organization strategy, every department and every team will have their own strategies that should augment and propel the overall strategy.

For instance, if a company has a relatively undersized marketing budget, it is the job of the head of marketing to create a strategy that maximizes the returns of those marketing dollars for the company. That strategy may then concentrate on digital marketing in only the top ten largest markets the company operates in or it could be to target only a particular customer segment (niche) that benefits most from being marketed to.

Now, tactics. Tactics are composed of the steps taken to achieve the strategy, the day-to-day and week-to-week operational plans and actions taken to work toward the mission. If you work in a small organization or a start-up company, you may engage in both the organizational strategy creation as well as tactics development. For mid and large-sized organizations, the creation of tactics occurs most at the individual and small-team level, while senior managers tend to drive the overall strategy.

For those who appreciate military analogies, strategy is to war as tactics are to battles.

What does all of this mean for you as a manager? Even as a junior manager engaged primarily on tactical decisions (and every level of manager above that), you should be thinking about strategy. You need to comprehend the broader strategies as much as possible in order to optimize the tactics. The more you can drive the strategy through good execution of the various pieces of which it is composed, the more you will be able to influence strategy, based on your performance and reputation.

Tactical insight can provide the means to winning the "war," so to speak. If a marketer develops a process to drive customers at 60% of the cost of competitors, through regular testing and optimization, that can be a big enough lever that it impacts the strategy of the larger department, if not the overall organization.

Comparative Strategy

To gain a solid understanding of the strategy of your team and your organization, it is useful to employ comparative reasoning (which is a fancy way of saying compare what you are doing to what others are doing):

- Compare your organization's strategy against its competitors. What makes your organization more or less successful than a competitor? What advantages does either side have that can be replicated and which ones cannot be copied (because of the time or cost required)?
- Has the organization been successful because of the strategy or despite itself because of the strengths in one area or larger macroeconomic factors? It seems great when an organization grows 10%, but if its competitors have all grown by 20% in the same period, 10% suddenly looks poor.
- Where is your organization or team focusing versus the competition? Are there certain niches of products,

services, or customers that your competitor specializes in, that you don't?

- Relate your division or team's strategy to the organization's strategy. How does it fit in and what is it meant to do to help achieve the organization's mission? Is it complementary to the broader strategy or at odds with it?
- How does the division / team strategy compare to counterparts in other organizations? Again, what makes the division or team better or worse than a competitor?
- Study what strategies other teams (e.g. marketing teams if you run a marketing team) in other industries (not your own industry) employ successfully.
- How do all of the above benefit or suffer from changes in: the economy, technology innovations, more competition, demographics, changes in price or supply, etc.?
- At each level, analyze the strengths and weaknesses of the strategy, as well as what elements the strategy focuses on. Trying to do everything well is not a strategy.

Outside of senior managers, this sort of analysis is rarely performed. Even managers who do this type of strategic legwork often do it only once a year as part of an annual plan. If that statement worries you, it should, because that means that most teams and organizations revisit strategies only once a year. The entire organization's infrastructure then builds around executing (even if not consciously) in yearly increments, and strategic projects become measured in quarters (of a year). This is a major reason for why start-ups can shake-up an entire industry, let alone topple individual competitors.

Study and analyze existing strategies in your industry (vertically) as well as similar functions across industries (horizontally). You will gain a much better sense of where your strategy falls relative to others in the same space.

Chapter 28: Creating a Nimble Strategy

Venture capitalists - the organizations that typically provide the first, large round of money to start-ups - quickly learn that ideas are a dime a dozen; it is the execution of ideas which matters. History is littered with amazing ideas that were simply not right for their time, didn't have enough resources, or were poorly developed.

Organizations that do a good job at focusing their resources on (even) an average strategy tend to do well. Superlative growth comes about when solid execution couples with a strong strategy. But what does it mean to have a strong strategy, and how do you build one?

Start first with the mission of the organization. The mission should define what is considered valuable. Is it more products sold? Funds raised? Users signed up? Errors reduced? Time saved? Figure out the value you need to propel, and you can assemble a strategy to foster that value.

What elements of your organization's strategy create a competitive advantage? Are there factors that benefit your team or do you need to come up with your own competitive advantages? What factor(s) of the strategy can you or do you need to change from the current state? Those types of factors include:

- The priorities of the strategy. Maybe price was the key focus of your team or its services / products and you need to compete on quality or speed.
- The focus of the strategy. Customers change, demographics change. Figure out where the opportunities lie.
- The discontinuation of elements that no longer work.

- The implementation of new technology and processes that become available.
- The development of new or unique internal operational processes.
- The initiation of new products or services or re-launching existing products and services updated for the current times.

Many organizations - and individuals - conduct a strategic assessment and end up creating a detailed, long-term strategy that looks good on paper, but ultimately falters in execution. When these massive strategies do pay off, they pay off well, but it is close to the odds of winning a lottery.

The world is changing only faster, not slower. All of the advances in technology and society are upending entire industries more and more rapidly. The mission of an organization might not change, but the strategy to achieve that mission must be reviewed and adjusted more frequently. Don't try to create a single perfect strategy that will last forever.

It is the ability to react more quickly than your competition to sudden changes and opportunities that often leads to success. Instead of a rarely changing semi-fixed strategy, create "nimble" strategies; strategies that adapt and shift to new requirements and scenarios.

Nimble strategies begin at the team level. If an organization's teams all begin to use nimble strategies that complement each other, the organization gains the ability to adapt as a whole much more quickly to enact larger positive changes.

To plan such nimble strategies:

1) **Keep aware of as many changes at the micro and macro level as possible.** Changes or developments in the various areas your team operates in (such as technology); changes in a competitor's team or organizational approach; changes in the industry (such as legislation).
2) **Constantly push yourself and your team to come up with new ideas internally.** They can be large or small, as long as they are not too large for you to try.
3) **Combine #1 and #2 to create unique strategies.**

4) **Develop a team and resources that can execute your strategy and pivot to new strategies.** That often means changes in resources, responsibilities, and new training for existing team members.

5) **Execute those strategies well.** It is all about the execution. It comes down to your team forming tactics and doing the work necessary to carry out the strategy. Every tactical decision your team makes should support the current strategy. That is the litmus test.

6) **Implement frequent, date-specific review cycles to assess the success or failure of the strategy.**

7) **Devote more resources to winners. Discard losers.** Which ideas, projects, or investments have created the most value?

8) **Develop competitive advantages where possible, which can give you a foundation.** Large dollar investments, proprietary knowledge, controlling resources, hiring the best people in the field, all of these allow you to sustain success for longer.

9) **Keep evolving the strategy, even - and particularly - when it is successful.** It is when you are successful that you can afford to take on more risk to try different strategies. If you don't keep evolving, you will eventually be superseded by someone else.

Figure out the highest level at which you can impact strategies. Perhaps that is at the level of your team; perhaps you have influence over the strategies of several teams in the organization that can drive greater change.

Translating Strategy into Tactics

At a certain point, you have to stop planning and start executing; over-planning is worse. Keep the idea of nimbleness and get going:

- **Share and explain all of the elements of the strategy with the entire team.** This unites everyone in a common purpose or understanding.
- **Create action plans for each functional area or unit within your team.** Involve your team members where

possible and give them items to execute on and deadlines in which to do so. Don't spend months developing action plans. If you have articulated a clear strategy, action plans can be devised in a week or two at the most. You can refine the details as you go along. The secret to successful strategies is actually implementing them.

- **Review action plans on a weekly, monthly, and quarterly basis.** Weekly reviews may only be with the people in charge of one particular area, but use the monthly and quarterly reviews to keep everyone in the loop.
- **Adjust the tactics when they aren't working, in real-time.** Don't allow yourself or your team to wait until scheduled reviews to adjust something if it isn't working. Either they adjust it themselves or they speak with you.
- **Adjust the strategy when the tactics work but the strategy does not.** The tactics may be sound, but perhaps your strategy isn't. For instance, a manufacturer's issue may not be the way it produces the product, but the fact that the product it is producing is not in demand.

These nimble strategies apply to entire organizations as much as teams, but teams can typically shift more quickly. If you can develop the ability to shift to new opportunities, you will realize outsized value, which will translate into surpassing established goals and expectations for your team. That creates success.

Chapter 29: Scaling Up & Failure Planning

You will never have a perfect record in anything you do over time. Some of the strategies, tactics, and methodologies that you implement will work well, and others will fail terribly. The trick is to take this as a fact of life and craft an approach that systematically scales (upward or outward) and puts more time in the things that work, while minimizing and controlling for the failures.

Scaling Systems & Processes

Anything that will be repeated, small or large, should be studied and systemized; processes for training your team, for executing regular requirements, for spending less time doing busy work and more time on work that drives results.

Too many groups – from three-person teams through organizations with twenty-thousand people – rely on what you could call "tribal knowledge." Tribal knowledge is the concept that a particular person or persons knows how to do something independent of protocol (for instance, the twenty steps involved in signing up a new customer) versus it being documented and standardized. A new team member can and does learn the steps from his or her peers, but it often happens in a non-organized way; for instance, a quick tutorial between two other tasks and no formal structure. Certainly, for some people that's enough to get the job done. But in a team of twenty people, you end up with fifteen slightly different ways of accomplishing that task; ways that vary in quality and time required.

As a top contributor, the challenge was to create and share standardizations in the work you do and the work shared with others. This is the kind of thinking and action that pulls you ahead of almost all of your peers. This kind of thinking will also vault you over many managers; only as a manager, you can put in place much broader systems and processes that you may not have been able to previously. Good leaders can not only come up with good solutions, but they more importantly have the power to implement them. Affect change in the larger roles you are given as a manager and you will continue to climb upward. This holds equally as true for an entrepreneur planning on growing his or her own business, as it does for someone working for a Fortune 500 company.

Standardize processes and training not only for common tasks, but also for the uncommon ones as well; the ones which only a few people carry out. Your goal is efficiency and continuity. That does not at all mean that your processes should be fixed in stone. Regularly update and tweak them and stay nimble. Just ensure that as you make updates, everything is documented and communicated. One warning, don't create efficiency in processes only to replace it with a large amount of work spent documenting that efficiency. Balance accordingly.

You aren't always going to have processes in place before the work needs to be done. There will be periods where you and your team have so much work to do that documenting and standardizing becomes a distant secondary goal. Resist the urge to cast systemization aside and make sure your team remembers that as well. If you are ever in doubt of the benefits of systemization, log all of the time and money that mistakes or the lack of clear processes cost, and you will quickly turn to systemization.

Plan for Failure

Hopefully, you fail small and fail frequently in order to continually improve and adapt to the requirements of a strategy and organization. That concept was covered in Part One and applies even more so when you are a manager who can implement many more testing scenarios for improvement and innovation.

Not all failures are small or planned. You will fail regularly in ways you didn't anticipate. Everyone does. Not horrible crashing failures that put you out of a job or out of business (though those of course can happen), but namely not hitting or achieving 100% of the many goals that are set by you or for you in a given period of time. You tell a client a piece of work will take three days, yet it takes five. When asked why it took five days, you waffle around without a short and clear answer. You expect your team to sell $500,000 worth of a product in a month and you sell $450,000. Not bad, but not the expectation. You work for a month on a project and your boss finds it to be worthless. These are common scenarios in which managers often have no alternative solution or explanation.

While you can't know every time you will fail in this way, you should expect that setbacks will happen. It is a great thing to plan for success, but you must also plan for failure and create contingency plans and responses for when you do fail. With every major action you take or goal you must attain, think about the various possible negative outcomes and the probability of those outcomes.

For all possible outcomes you can anticipate, plan ways to lessen their impact or decrease the likelihood of a negative outcome happening. Set your internal or individual goals higher than the expectation. Give yourself some padding in the resources required to get the job done. Enact better internal review processes. Every situation has a way to limit potential downside, as well as a way to deal with whatever downside still ensues.

Communication is often the least cited but most important element of acknowledging failure and reducing its impact. The less time between an incident and everyone affected, the more easily everyone can come up with strategies to mitigate or fix the problem. If you can do nothing else, communicate quickly.

When you have a situation that you can't mitigate the impact of, at least be proactive and come up with a proposed solution to keep it from happening or decrease its impact the next time it occurs. A mistake the first time is likely forgiven; the same mistake repeated over and over generates worse consequences.

By planning for multiple outcomes, good and bad, you will also train yourself to be more nimble and have an easier time making faster decisions. A manager has to make dozens of decisions every day that have varying levels of impact on the future. Part of having a good track record is not assuming that every decision will turn out perfect, but having a plan for the results of bad decisions as well.

Section Four: Building Your Team

In most management roles, you are expected to supervise other people. The majority of managers have little-to-no formal management education and lack strong mentors to help them develop. As with other types of skills, there are natural leaders and managers who intuitively grasp the essentials, but everyone benefits from focused training.

Many people underestimate the importance and value of good management compared to average management, until they see the difference in the results that a good manager can produce with the same resources given to an average manager. The following outcomes are typical:

- An average manager with an average team will produce average results.
- An average manager with a good team will produce good results at first but often drives the team to become average over time.
- A good manager with an average team will shape his or her people into a good team over time.
- A good manager with a good team produces amazing results.

Is there any question as to what type of team you would want to be a part of? This section focuses on creating an environment that supports great teams and the necessary steps to build those teams.

Chapter 30: The Philosophy of Hiring

I've had to hire for about eighty positions in my own career to date. On average, each posted position has seen fifty resumes sent in, seven or eight phone interviews, and three to four in-person interviews before I have made a hiring decision. Crunching the numbers, that comes to roughly 4,000 resumes, 560 phone calls, and 250 in-person interviews. To some of you reading this, those may sound like small numbers, especially if you are in a recruiting position. Other readers may think these are large figures, if you haven't hired before or rely on your HR department to do much of the initial screening. The main reason I share these statistics isn't to impress, but to provide a basis for why I have spent so much time weeding through resumes and conducting interviews.

Hiring a person is one of the biggest decisions you make in any given month, or even year. People that execute work for you and who think of things you haven't are immensely valuable. No matter how smart you are, an army of one only goes so far. To scale your accomplishments larger and larger, you need a great set of people working with you and supporting you. Your ability to consistently hire good people lets you build momentum with your results and build confidence in removing poor contributors from your team.

The decisive factor to success as a supervising manager condenses to this: hire the people who are as smart as possible yet work well with others, then give them the opportunity to flourish. Underline and circle that sentence. If you think that being stuck constantly supervising every detail of your team's work and behavior is fun, you haven't tried it. It means long hours, a lot of a stress, and constant setbacks. Hire great people and you can make big steps forward.

How do you methodically hire great people? It is worth looking at the average hiring process to understand its gaps.

Why is it that among so many different types of industries, roles, and organizations that hiring processes are so depressingly similar? The average hiring process follows a pretty set process: post on major job boards, screen resumes, conduct interviews (first phone and then in-person), and make an offer to who is thought to be the best candidate interviewed. The process suffers from common issues such as:

- Generic job posting that looks like every other organization's posting for a position.
- Incomplete pools of candidates apply for the positions, as the best performers / players often aren't checking job listings.
- Great potential applicants missed because resume readers, hiring for 20 different positions, are simply scanning for certain keywords, not reading the resumes with insight.
- Phone and in-person interviews conducted by people without a background in the area (this doesn't matter as much in some positions, but a heck of a lot for specialized / technical positions).
- A candidate's charm and ability to sweet-talk the interviewers often gets him or her the position, as reference checks (real reference checks, not just verifications of work history) are often not conducted.
- One, sometimes two, interviews average with a candidate before they are offered a position; selections are made from fairly small pools of candidates because of an impatience to fill the position.

To be clear on one point, the blame for this does not fall on Human Resources (HR) departments. A great HR department is much more critical to the long-term success of an organization than most give credit for. Many HR departments are ignored, seen simply as the places to do the basics of job posting, assisting in the hiring process, managing employee issues, and complying with labor laws. Organizations who make large investments in HR personnel (who are "rock stars") receive a pay-off a hundred times over.

This section presents a model for hiring, from beginning to end, that produces better results. The guiding factor behind every element is a desire to hire the best possible people. It is a fluid process that adapts and changes based on the different types of positions out there and the unique requirements of each. Regardless of whether you are hiring at a fast food restaurant or a law office, the underlying principles remain the same.

Here are the essential steps to hiring, each of which has a chapter that explores it in more detail:

1) Understand & Define the Position You are Hiring for
2) Build a Funnel of All Possible Qualified Candidates
3) Resume Screening
4) Screening Tools to Boil Down Candidates
5) Interview Tips & Tricks
6) Structuring the Offer
7) Reference Checks

Done with proper care and execution, you will develop the methods to ensure that you receive a steady flow of high-quality candidates that allow you to build a great team.

Chapter 31: Understand & Define the Position You Are Hiring for

Before you or an HR specialist posts a job advertisement, take the time to define the ideal candidate for the position. If the position has been filled previously, take a fresh look at whether previous candidates have been successful or if you have not attracted the right people to the position historically.

What combination of skills, attributes, and experience would make for an ideal hire? Catalogue the technical / hard skills and organizational skills that someone filling the position must have. Then separately catalogue any managerial experience required. Do you know any person - directly or indirectly - within your organization or outside of it that can serve as the model example of a candidate for the role?

The type of position also dictates the approach you should take during the hiring process to identify the best candidates. There are two primary groups that require different approaches:

Job Group #1: This group is composed of positions where the screening and interview process are the central factors in evaluating a candidate. That can be because candidates don't have a long track record / experience in a particular field or industry; or their jobs are based on certain skillsets that must be assessed, regardless of length of experience.

Job Group #2: This group encompasses positions where the hiring decision is made more on the candidate's track record in previous jobs. It is a different dynamic to hire people from Group #2, especially if / when you begin hiring for more senior positions. You aren't going to have a senior manager run through the same hiring process as someone just out of high school or college.

Breaking down candidates into one of the two groups clarifies the direction of hiring for that particular position versus a one-size-fits-all approach.

Job Group #1 - Hires Based on the Interview / Screening Process

Technical-skill based positions, as well as positions you wish to fill with people freshly out of school, fall into this category.

Most positions in Job Group #1 will give you a problem of having too many applicants to sift through.

A related problem: how do you determine which candidates really have the actual caliber of technical or organizational skills that they put on their resumes? For example, in the design world, there are only a few major programs that designers use in their work. Everyone writes that they are "proficient" or "great" with these programs. But they are complex pieces of software that really take a lot of time and dedication to learn the more advanced workings of; a manager without that technical experience isn't going to know off-hand how to evaluate that.

Candidates who are just beginning their careers often lack the historical work experience to draw insight from. What else do you use to make an appraisal?

Less experienced candidates will also require a larger amount of training and supervision, at least initially. You need to be aware of that, if that's the case, and make provisions for that type of support. If you hire someone that requires training and fail to provide that training, it is largely your fault that they have failed.

Job Group #2 - Hires Based on a Reputation / Strong Track Record

After a certain level, hiring becomes less about a complex screening process early on and more about finding people who already have a track record of success. Odds are they will keep having successes if they are given the resources they need. Seniority is a relative concept. For certain positions, two years of work signifies expertise. For other positions, twenty years might be the number.

Your evaluations will focus on digging into their stated achievements and accomplishments, via their own words, their references, and anything they can point to and claim as their own.

If it is a supervisory position, it expands to assessing a person's ability to build their own team and cultivate talent.

As opposed to the first group, you will typically see too few qualified candidates apply for the position. This dictates a more aggressive approach to finding candidates.

For the more experienced candidates in Group #2, there is another consideration: they aren't going to change very much after a certain point in their career. If you take a director with twenty years of experience and place him or her in a new position, you must accept the fact that you won't be able to impact much about his or her approach, especially in the short-term. He or she will have developed his or her own methods of completing the work and / or managing the work. The fit of the organization to the person, and the person to the organization, and their mutual understanding of each other, must be properly evaluated before an offer is made and that offer is accepted. Managing expectations for both sides is critical.

Wildcard Hires

Both Groups #1 and #2 mostly assume that you are hiring a person who wants a specific role or has the experience performing that role already. But there is also the notion of a "wildcard hire," someone who has many positive traits and does good work, but lacks a direct background in an area. Hires made directly out of college have some of this characteristic, as while you can look for promising traits, you still have little prior history on which to make a decision.

Senior positions also allow for wildcard hires. Some of the largest organizational successes come from industry outsiders; those who haven't worked in the specific field, those who apply knowledge from other areas into a static field, those who break the pre-established limits in an area because they didn't know those limits existed, or those who dare to be bold enough to intentionally break those limits. When successful, these types of people create large, positive changes on a team and organization.

The point of mentioning wildcard hires here is that you must decide whether you want to consider them during the hiring process. If you do have an HR department doing initial interview screening for you, candidates that don't fit the stated requirements of the job may be screened out immediately if they don't fit into the exact bounds you have stated. You may have stipulated three

Succeed Big Professionally

years' experience in radio advertising as a position requirement, which causes the reviewer to immediately exclude a person with only two years' experience in radio advertising but extraordinarily strong results. Wildcard hires will require more work to sift through and assess, but they can work out very, very well. If you have others assisting you with the hiring process, and you do decide to consider wildcards, it is your responsibility to make those helping you aware of that and show them what types of candidates you are willing to consider.

One especially good place to consider wildcard hires is for positions where there have been a string of unsuccessful people in the role, and it makes sense to break the mold and find someone who might take a different approach.

As the manager / hiring party, you should think about whether a position can afford the risk of hiring a wildcard; the rewards can be great, but you must consider what the particular cons are in hiring that wildcard.

Industry outsiders are a common type of wildcard hire. A sales manager who has had great success in industry X might very well do an amazing job in industry Y. But that sales manager might be more likely to fail in industry Y if there is a requirement that the position has a real depth and expertise in the industry; depth that takes years to acquire. You will have to accept that there will be a learning curve for a wildcard hire. As long as the pain of the learning curve is acceptable to you, the organization, vendors, or customers, it may well be worth it.

A second type of wildcard hire: someone drawn from inside of the same organization, who doesn't have a direct background in the open position. They have proven themselves in other roles and they are now felt to be the right choice to reinvigorate or rebuild the area. Like the first type of wildcard candidate, he or she will have a learning curve in that particular role. However, these candidates do come with the benefit of knowing the overall organizational strategy, which helps to align focus. If it is a managerial position, it goes back to whether the candidate is good at both strategy development and team-building.

A good hiring process goes beyond simply listing out the years of experience and skills that you are looking for. Obtain a nuanced understanding of the requirements of the position and the types of people that can succeed in it. That knowledge will greatly increase your odds of knowing where to find the right candidates, and the best ways to attract them.

Chapter 32: Structuring the Position & Opportunity

You can identify the perfect type of person for a role, but do you have the ability to attract that person to your organization?

In a perfect world, you have a fast-growing organization with a stellar reputation that everyone wants to work for, and enough money to pay whatever the top candidates desire for the position. For the extremely rare Googles of the world, that's possible. For most other organizations, certain limits will exist. It is your job to understand those limits; not to simply stay within them, but to also find ways around them.

Some people will apply to any open job because they need to (mostly common for financial reasons) or haven't thought carefully about a career path. The elements of a job that attract a more discerning person are:

- A good / high salary and benefits.
- Responsibilities of the position (day to day work).
- Opportunities for a promotion.
- Ability to develop new skills and abilities (professional growth).
- The reputation / brand of the organization.
- A fun and supportive company culture / work environment.

It falls on you to properly research and consider the following:

- The reputation and track record of your organization versus others.
- The compensation you can offer versus what the competitor with the deepest pockets can offer.
- The limiting factors such as geographical location and specialty skills required that will make the candidate pool small.
- The opportunity for growth and advancement that the position offers.
- The positives you can offer or create that offset any negatives.

Make a realistic assessment of what your limitations are and which ones you can get around versus not.

Some limits may be inflexible, such as location. Your organization may be isolated from the broader talent pool for that position, which limits the amount of good candidates. But perhaps you can offer a certain rural lifestyle to a candidate seeking it. Perhaps you can afford to pay slightly more than some competitors. The "how" of getting past the limit is what's important.

Compensation is sometimes flexible, sometimes not. Some organizations don't allow junior and middle-level managers to set a compensation range. Because of this, it may be that you can pay up to $45,000 for a candidate, but no higher. Yet, your competitor pays $50,000. It's your job as a manager to research the average compensation for roles you hire for, craft budgets, and operate within the framework of the organization to make a case for paying what you need to in order to get the right talent. Here, the point is that if you are paying less than your competitors, it will reduce the amount of top candidates who will accept job offers.

When you understand where you can customize benefits that your competition does not have, as well as the limits you can't overcome, you create a realistic hiring scenario. Multiple amazing candidates exist for most positions; they all have different combinations of personal and professional goals. Your position may not appeal to all of the top candidates with its limitations, but when properly planned, it will appeal to at least some of the top candidates. That's critical.

The Job Posting

With a hiring scenario created, you arrive at a target and maximum possible compensation package, you know how much your organization's reputation helps or hinders your ability to hire, and you have figured out the intangible benefits you can offer. You can now create a job posting that appeals to the pool of candidates that you both want to hire and can realistically be able to hire.

Generic descriptions will yield generic results. Tailored job descriptions will yield great candidates. Postings that speak to why the organization or the team is great to work with, and why the best candidates should consider it, make a huge difference.

Study ten different job postings for the same position in different organizations. Nine of the ten will read almost exactly the same.

Spend the time yourself or with your HR department crafting job postings that stand out from the competition. At the minimum you should have:

- A captivating headline different from your competitors.
- An introduction that gives real flavor to the position and the opportunities - professional, financial, or personal - that come with it.
- A carefully written, dynamic description of the organization. Not a generic, "company ABC is a [fill in the blank company] in the [fill in the blank industry]." Highlight the strengths of the organization and what makes it great to work there.
- Be specific as to the ideal candidate for the position, as well as the acceptable types of applicants.

Use the job posting to paint a compelling picture. Great candidates will be drawn to the postings that stand out. Everything that highlights the opportunity and builds your hiring funnel is gold.

Chapter 33: Build a Funnel of All Possible Qualified Candidates

"Build it and they will come", or "post it and they will come" is not a wonderful method of attracting the best talent. A select few organizations have the brand or prestige to have the top talent constantly attuned to possible openings. The rest, though, can't expect every - or even a few - of the stellar candidates out there to apply for every position. Some of these great candidates may be on the market because they are dissatisfied with their current position or need to make a change for personal reasons. But most already have a position elsewhere in which they are making their mark; they need to be made aware of the opportunity. First, that the opportunity exists, and second, why the opportunity is right for them. It is evident to say that you want every great candidate to apply for your position. But you have to do the work to get there.

The typical scenario for driving awareness of a position opening involves posting to the major job boards or newspapers. The manager of the team and people connected to the organization also toss out a few candidates based on connections and relationships.

To improve and really build the funnel of prospective candidates, go further:

- Post with specialist job boards and trade associations (many industries and specialties these days have dedicated niches). Weigh the costs of each channel and try as many as possible.
- Use your website and communications channels - like social media and newsletters - to mention job openings.

The people who already know your brand in some way may be wonderful candidates.

- Spread word of the listing internally, especially among different managers (in bigger organizations) to identify internal candidates. This isn't done as often or as methodically as you might initially think. Contractors are also a source of great talent. You may have someone who has worked with the organization part-time for months or years, who knows the nuances of the organization, is well-liked, and could be a great permanent contributor.
- Actively recruit for the best candidates, either yourself or with the help of HR.
- Leverage peer referrals. Peer referrals work.

Hiring from Within

Long-term, you want to establish a culture of cultivating talent internally; talent that knows and understands the culture and mission of the organization already. Done well, you can leverage a large stream of qualified men and women who will have a higher likelihood of being successful in a new role than an outsider who must contend with a completely new environment. That does not mean that insiders are always the perfect answer; sometimes an organization becomes so focused internally on how great it is or in a method of accomplishing things, that external opportunities are lost and new perspectives are rarely considered.

Internal candidates should go through the same hiring process as external ones, save for the fact that you have to worry less about not knowing their actual contributions or ability to work with others. That in and of itself is a huge benefit.

Hiring from within regularly sends a strong message to all of the talented people in your organization that there are opportunities for advancement for those who showcase superior results and have the drive and desire to continue making progress in their career paths.

Active Recruitment

For any position for which the target candidate pool will already be small, you should establish processes to go after the best seeds. Someone needs to be tasked first with posting the job ad with the standard sources, and then with using the job requirements and description to hunt for candidates who seem promising but haven't applied. LinkedIn particularly is an invaluable recruitment tool that allows you to search for specific types of roles / experience and read through a person's work history. More old-fashioned approaches work well too. Research the field and competitors, compile a list, and start contacting them. The vast majority of people don't mind being solicited regarding a job position if you are polite and non-aggressive about it. If they have no interest, move on. If they do, you have gained another viable candidate.

External recruiters also have their place in helping source specialized positions; mostly those who have deep networks for certain specialty roles, or for organizations that truly don't have the bandwidth to do active recruiting internally. However, many organizations get into a poor habit of kicking a position to an external recruiter to fill after a month of doing little more than having posted a job ad. Do what you and your organization can to fill the position via all of the above channels first, and only then utilize external resources. Given how important it is to hire exceptional people, make the investments in time and structure to allow you to source the best candidates yourself.

Peer Referrals

Harness the power of your team or organization in helping to find qualified applicants. Every year, a large number of new employees are sourced from the current employees of an organization. A current employee sits at a great crossroad of knowing the organization's values, goals, and culture, while being acquainted with people outside of the organization who might be looking for a new position. Good people often know other good people, so it is a strong bet that a star employee has friends or acquaintances that might be suitable for a particular role. A talented current employee will also be pretty selective in who he or she refers for a position, as they know that applicant's interview process and performance in the organization (if hired) will reflect on their referral; it is a great natural filter.

There aren't many downsides to the process of peer referrals. Candidates referred by a peer shouldn't get a pass through all of the various hiring stages. You can start them off wherever in the hiring cycle you prefer, such as a phone-interview and proceed from there if they do well.

You should make it clear to the employee who made the referral that his or her reference is not a guarantee that the friend / acquaintance will be hired. You should also make sure that the referring employee realizes that being someone's friend, versus working with them day-in and day-out, can be a test of that familiarity with one another.

Never allow a manager to hire a real friend as a subordinate. Friendship and the manager-subordinate role do not play well together. If ever a disagreement arises, friendship can cloud judgement on both sides. If that new employee does not end up being a rock star, cries of favoritism will rise up.

Referrals by another member in your organization, such as a different team leader, a supervisor, or from one of your mentors, are also a great way of finding candidates, as long as you stick to your entire vetting process with those referred. You should make it clear to everyone that you don't hire solely based on someone else's recommendation, but always evaluate candidates based on your own hiring cycle and decisions.

If your organization does give a hiring bonus to any employee whose referral results in a hire, bravo; it will serve you well. If no such hiring bonus exists, it is the sort of conversation to bring up with your own supervisor or HR department as something to investigate. Posting an ad on the major job boards for just a few months will typically cost over $1,000. Consider utilizing that money first as a hiring bonus, before marketing the position externally. A lack of a hiring bonus policy won't cripple peer job referrals, but it certainly shows a current employee that the organization values their contribution.

If you cast a truly wide net out to every possible qualified candidate, whether they are actively looking for a new position or not, you give yourself much higher odds of finding a great addition to your team.

Chapter 34: Resume Screening

Resumes carry the sum of a person's history in a few pages. Some hiring managers dislike digging through resumes, but they are extremely useful insofar that there is a near-universal expectation to provide a resume as part of the application process. Most everyone is told that a good resume is extremely important. If there is that expectation, it seems fair then that you should be able to carefully judge a resume as an initial step in understanding a candidate and his or her abilities. But what specifically to look for (or not) in assessing a resume?

There is a list of things to watch out for, either as positive indicators or negative flags:

Current skill level. What is the candidate's current skill level and how does that compare with other candidates? For instance, if you are looking at a resume of an engineer two years out of college, does his or her skill level and produced work seem like what you would expect, or is it better than most senior engineers?

Progression of responsibilities & results. This applies more to candidates with 5+ years of experience. In those cases, is there an upward trend over time in his or her job function, title, duties, and results? Or a person may have the same title for a decade; but over that period do they showcase a development of knowledge and contributions that separate him or her from someone with less experience?

How someone talks about his or her experience and results in his or her positions. The resume is meant to be a distillation of someone's career. So take it to be an example of the best facts that a candidate can produce. Granted, some men and women talk about their history poorly and otherwise can be great additions to the team. If you are hiring for a position that requires excellent communication skills (many do), pay attention to how a candidate phrases things. Generic phrases such as "key contributor to the team's sales strategy" or "managed a team" might signal that the candidate didn't actually make many specific contributions, and it doesn't tell anything about how good or bad he or she was at doing those things. When you have three or four bullet points (on average) to explain what you have done in a particular position, and the best you provide is a generic statement, it isn't going to impress someone. Part One of the book contains a model for resume writing; in reading a resume, look for how well a candidate sums up their contributions in a role with specific detail.

Tenure in positions. For candidates right out of school, this doesn't apply, but after someone has been working for more than two years, look at how long they have been in each position. Avoid "resume jumpers", people who can't seem to hold a job longer than a year (or less), job after job. Whether they have professional issues or regular personal ones, it is a cause for concern. It takes months on average to get a new hire to their full potential contribution, learning the nuances of a new position. You don't want to make that sort of investment in someone who seems to have a pattern of exiting organizations quickly. There are many valid reasons for leaving an organization, but it is about the reasons why and looking for patterns of behavior.

Additional relevant history. Many people include a section that talks about their major hobbies and efforts outside of their primary job, such as non-profit work, or clubs and associations they belong to. Younger candidates may include time spent playing on high school or college sports teams. If it is generically written, you can't count it as a plus, but some candidates demonstrate strong results in these sections, especially in terms of leadership activities. A commonly good indicator is when a candidate achieves a leadership position in a peer-driven environment, such as intramural sports. These men and women gain those positions by getting the support of all of their peers as the best person to lead the team or group. That suggests clear, logical communication skills, focus, and potential management savvy.

Typos. The average resume is one to two pages. If it is meant to highlight a candidate in a few short pages, you should expect it to be free of typos, especially misspellings. In the age of spell-check, it boggles the mind as to how many resumes are still sent with these types of errors, where it seems the person didn't proof a resume or even run spell-check. That suggests a lack of attention to detail and carelessness.

Generic "key strengths" and introductory sentence sections. Many resumes contain a set of bullet points or sentences that talk about what a candidate brings to the table. Most are very boilerplate, using phrases such as "top performer", "strategic planning", "effective communication", "good time manager", "high energy", or "extensive sales experience". Think about it this way: did you ever hear someone talk about him or herself and say "I'm a very average candidate"? Everyone describes themselves as a great performer and contributor. You want to be able to read specifically about what they have done that displays real excellence; if this section lacks such specifics, ignore it.

Education. In someone's first few years after college, their alma mater may matter. Some schools have a reputation for producing sharp thinkers, good salespeople, etc. Similar logic applies for graduate schools. But after those initial years, the school tends to matter less than the other items mentioned above. Candidates who attended the best universities can exhibit very average results and candidates who didn't go to the best schools present amazing track records in their professional careers. Obviously if the position requires certain technical degrees or certifications, you should do your own homework on the institution and the candidate's knowledge. Otherwise, base more of your judgment on what the candidate has achieved professionally.

Fancy resume designs and structures. If hiring for a creative position, a creatively designed resume can add a nice touch, but some candidates go too far, and create a visually confusing document. Judge accordingly.

All of the above may seem like a lot to evaluate, but once you become accustomed to reading through resumes, it takes just a minute or two to make an initial assessment. You then set aside good resumes for deeper reading.

This stage of the hiring process also encompasses reviewing any pertinent work examples (for applicable positions). For example, if you are hiring a writer or architect, you should request examples of their work to be included with the resume. In certain cases going through work examples will give you a much clearer sense of a candidate's potential than their resume.

Trust yourself and be patient. It seems pretty clear at first: if you don't have a fantastic candidate that you absolutely love for a position, don't hire him or her. Often though, as a position sits vacant, a manager loses patience. Don't fall prey to this. Be patient.

Many hiring mistakes are made when a manager becomes a little desperate to fill the position and begins considering resumes and candidates they wouldn't otherwise consider because they want someone in that role. Don't do it. You will always regret hiring an average candidate versus having waited for the best person for that role. Spread the work around in the team, use contractors or short-term labor, but don't sacrifice on quality.

Chapter 35: Screening Tools to Boil Down Candidates

You have a large number of resumes that seem promising for the position. Now you move on to interviews. Or do you?

For candidates who don't have long track records, or who have technical skills that must be ascertained, the use of screening questions is very helpful. It is harder to utilize these tools for positions in Job Group #2 (see Chapter 31), as the candidates' track records establish the baseline, and most senior candidates would scoff at the idea of answering written questions or taking tests when their achievements sell them.

Some organizations use screening tools to weed out the unqualified applicants as part of the initial job application, and others leverage screening tools after qualified candidates have been identified. One cautionary note: even good candidates may initially be hesitant to spend a chunk of time in a screening process unless they feel they have some possibility of getting the position.

Screening tools can simply ensure a base level of understanding of certain skills or values, or you can use them to separate average skills and average thinking from superlative skills and strategic thinking.

Many types of screening tools exist. They can be deployed before interviews, during phone interviews, or during on-site interviews. The lines can blur a bit between screening tools and questions you ask a candidate during an interview (as the entire process of hiring someone is one big screening), but try to define screening tools as a methodical set of questions or tasks that measure each candidate in the same way. Some organizations have automated testing tools for positions, such as software programming tests that require live coding, or they may have a machinist applicant actually run a machine or mill a sample to gauge his or her abilities.

Don't feel like you have to spend weeks developing screening tools. For example, it can be as basic yet effective as designing and sending two to four questions to applicants. The questions are constructed to require critical thinking, pulled from the types of scenarios that a candidate would encounter in a position. They are not simple questions (those are best to pose in-person, away from the easy answers provided by a search engine) that can be quickly researched. Tell candidates there is no time minimum or maximum, within reason; they may spend a couple of days to send back answers, and have the latitude to spend as much or as little time completing them as they feel appropriate.

Of those responses that you do receive back, there will be a full range: great responses back quickly, poor responses that someone spent a full day on, great responses that indicate a large amount of research, etc. All of these tell quite a detailed story not only about how a candidate thinks, but in those cases where they might not know an answer immediately and have done deep research, it suggests a strong desire for the position and a trait of tenacity.

A very small amount of candidates may reply to you and say they don't want to answer the questions because they have their own "proprietary" method or don't want to give their "great ideas" away. If a person feels that answering a few questions really gives away something magical, they either have very few good ideas, or they should go start their own company based on those ideas (if they are really that good). Look for consistent contributors, not one-hit wonders.

There are candidates who will simply never reply to you after being sent the screening questions. Typically, they either see the questions and don't think they can answer them well or don't want to spend the time answering them. In either case, the positives outweigh the negatives if you are looking for sharp, hungry contributors to add to your team or organization. The other great benefit of using this process is that it does allow for assessing wildcard candidates with an equal slate. Some of your best hires could be those with little background in the space, who had resumes that barely warranted consideration or weren't quite right, but really shined in answering the screening questions.

One last note. In cases where you have a candidate referred by an existing employee, the only "pass" you should give the candidate is on a weak or average resume. You can still allow them to answer the screening questions, but no one should get a pass on those questions. You don't want to take shortcuts in a process that works. Either apply it to all candidates or none.

Chapter 36: Structuring Useful Interviews

As you compile a short list of candidates that seem suited for the position (and / or have passed any screening scenarios), it becomes time to conduct interviews.

(Newer) managers: You are going to mess up with the first set of candidates that you evaluate. Even managers with plenty of experience under their belts are rough when they recruit for a new position that they haven't hired for before. Save your phone interviews and in-person interviews for the "best" candidates on your list until after you have spoken to a few other candidates. As with most things in life, there is a learning curve. Average candidates will not only give you a baseline, they will also let you figure out questions and considerations that you may wish to employ in the assessment process that you might not have thought of previously. In every new position you hire for, you will think of new questions in the dialogue with a candidate that suddenly seems critical to ask of all candidates as they help you hone in on a desirable trait or indicator of fit.

Whether it be phone interviews, in-person interviews, or a combination thereof, a number of options exist for how to structure the interview process. It will depend on the type of position you are hiring for. Some positions, for instance those in the food service or retail industries, opt to take their short list of candidates and schedule half or full-day hiring sessions where they conduct 20 to 30-minute in-person interviews with each candidate. Other organizations swear by using phone interviews first, to wean down the list of candidates; those who pass the phone interview stage are invited to the office for the next round.

You can add additional layers by conducting multiple phone interviews before extending invitations for in-person interviews.

You can also opt to do multiple rounds of in-person interviews. Experiment with different processes to find a combination which works best for you and the requirements of the position.

Phone Interviews

A key function of the phone interview can and should be telling the candidate more about the organization, team, position, and answering their questions. It is really unfortunate (and the hiring manager's fault) when a candidate goes all the way through a series of phone and in-person interviews only to find out near the end of the process that the job expectations are different from what they initially thought, or that the salary of the position differs radically from expectations. Use the phone interview to first cycle through your questions, and then to ensure the candidate has all of the information.

The manager to whom the candidate would report can conduct one phone interview as the primary, and then involve other members in the team or organization as secondary interviewers. These ancillary phone interviews allow for additional perspectives on the candidate, as well as giving the candidate multiple perspectives on the position, team, and organization.

If you do choose to employ phone interviews, you further whittle down your list of candidates to those who you wish to invite to in-person sessions. You can be aggressive with candidates and extend that invitation at the end of the phone interview, or let them know that they will hear from you in the next few days after you have spoken with other candidates. That gives you flexibility to weigh candidates against each other. You will often have a different perspective in the first few candidates you talk to for any given position. Give yourself time to develop clarity and not make snap judgements. Conversely, don't wait more than a week to extend that invitation, as strong candidates are likely exploring other opportunities as well. Losing a great candidate to another organization is quite painful. Be transparent and manage expectations.

In-Person Interviews

In-person interviews have four uses:

- To expose the candidate to more people in the organization face-to-face (for the benefit of both sides).
- To delve into questions and scenarios with the candidate on their technical abilities, soft skills, and management traits.
- To educate the candidate more about the position and organization.
- To ascertain culture fit with the team and organization.

You might conduct only one phone interview, but decide to have the candidate participate in three or four one-on-one interviews with different people in the organization.

The structure of the interviews can vary. When the candidate sits down with you in-person after having passed a phone interview, ostensibly you are going to have different / deeper questions for him or her. Some of the other interviews can focus more on one particular aspect of a candidate, such as his or her analytical skills, technical skills, culture fit, or management ability. For instance, a candidate for a clinical position might sit down with another similar clinician in the organization and have an in-depth discussion on clinical approaches. Or a candidate might meet with the supervisor's boss, with the point of the interview being to gauge cultural fit and see if any flags pop up.

Related to the focus of the interview are the types of people with whom you have the candidate additionally interview. There are a number of options:

- You (their potential manager)
- Their future peers
- Their future direct reports (the people who would report to the candidate if hired, relevant for manager-level positions)
- Other peers in the organization that hold a similar position
- Your boss
- Other managers in the organization

Besides one-on-one interviews, consider group interviews, especially for a more casual setting where a broader team can talk informally with a candidate, and both sides can get a sense of whether or not they like each other.

Peer Interviews

Peer interviews should be a core part of the interview process, by phone and / or in-person. True peer interviews exclude you (the manager) or any other person seen as "management." They serve very well in three ways: Seeing a person's true personality, their way of thinking, and giving your team experience in the hiring process (a later chapter addresses the last point in greater depth).

Regarding a person's true personality, many job candidates are going to be very formal in the way they speak, as well as what they say, with their potential boss. They tend to relax around someone they see as being closer to their level. Sometimes this is an upside surprise, where they actually shine more when comfortable; other times, it can reveal negative characteristics that they hid in their interactions with you.

Every person has a different personality, different ways in which he or she approaches problems and decision-making, and different ways of working with a team or clients. Given that working with others as a team is such a critical trait, the way a candidate communicates with a potential future team member can speak volumes. It helps both sides to understand if there is a fit in the style of communication, accountability, and decision-making.

Everyone who conducts interviews is not going to agree every time on who is best for a position. It is rare that they all agree, and there are going to be cases where you, as a manager, feel that the team is missing some key quality a candidate could bring to the table. (Don't read that as you being perfect; even the best hiring managers' track records have strikes.)

You also don't want to hire the exact same type of person (or personality) every time, as you lose valuable competing perspectives. A candidate that challenges others in a productive way can introduce a new, positive dynamic and fresh insights.

When possible, you should never be the only person making a decision on a hire because you will miss positives or negatives that others may not. It is worth stressing as, commonly, some managers do make hiring decisions without consulting others; these types of hires turn out badly more frequently than not, especially when it emerges that they don't or can't work well with the team, carry different expectations, etc. To be clear, the hiring decision should always be yours, but soliciting other's feedback is a good habit.

Create a structured process that is comprehensive and allows you to identify the best possible candidates for a position. Does conducting extra sets of interviews seem like unnecessary work? It isn't when you run the numbers. What is an extra 30 minutes here or 30 minutes there of engaging with a candidate that will work 40 or more hours a week for you, the team, and organization? That's over 2000 hours in any given year. A small investment up front can greatly increase your chances of a good decision.

Interview Questions

Structures aside, what questions do you ask for phone and / or in-person interviews?

Technical questions. If you are hiring for a role that requires specific skills or knowledge, you'll be asking these sorts of questions. Given the thousands of types of jobs out there, this book can't go into specifics. Do be thorough to ensure the candidate possesses the required skills. An unfortunately common and critical mistake, especially in managers (or an HR representative) hiring for a specialist role they have never done themselves, is to fail to adequately assess a candidate's technical skills. If you don't have the background yourself in a technical skill that you need to assess, find someone within or outside of the organization who can ask the right questions to conduct a good assessment.

Background and experience questions. A rich source of questions - especially in the first rounds of speaking with a candidate - can be pulled from his or her resume and other provided information.

- Have candidates talk in detail about the achievements from previous positions that they listed in their resume. This may seem basic or obvious, but you gain a lot more color than the sentence-or-two description from the resume. That color can drastically change your opinion about the value of that achievement or contribution, up or down. Some candidates overstate their contribution to an impressive accomplishment their previous team or organization achieved. If they did as much as they say they did in their resume, they should be easily able to speak to those accomplishments in detail.
- Ask candidates to tell you the piece of work they did that had the greatest contribution or was the most innovative,

for each of the major positions that they have previously held. You might be surprised by how many can't come up with a good, specific answer. Great candidates always ace this question though, as they quickly point to multiple things that they contributed to which separated them from their peers or made a big difference for the organization.

- Why did they leave previous positions, especially the most recent ones? Make sure you feel satisfied with the answers. "It wasn't a good fit" is a generic answer. Figure out if a candidate left because the work wasn't challenging enough, because of professional reasons (including if it was a voluntary departure or they were fired), or personal issues. The decision to leave an organization is a big one that will tell you a good deal about him or her.

- Address holes or deficits you see in experience. Candidates may meet most, but not all, of your criteria. Question them on how they see themselves making up for those deficits or learning what is necessary for the position quickly. You can then make decisions based on those answers and the resources you have to train them or otherwise make up for the gaps.

Critical thinking and logic questions. Some organizations use questions completely unrelated to the position to gauge how someone thinks in real-time. Those types of questions are fun (such as, "Why are manhole covers round?") but don't necessarily tell you how a candidate will deal with actual problems or scenarios he or she will face in that position. You will learn much more by posing questions based on actual scenarios or decisions a candidate would have to make. Those questions can be simple or complex. As with the technical questions, you may want to source some of these from an expert in the subject if you are not one yourself, or have such an expert conduct one of the interviews with the candidate. Pull from actual problems that have been solved. Have a baseline for acceptable responses and, of course, look for great responses. For roles that require strategy development, make sure to ask not only tactical (day-to-day decision-making questions), but strategic (long-term planning and larger decision) questions. Examples in this category:

- A customer comes in with a problem about [fill in the blank]. What do you say or do?
- What will your six-month strategy be to drive results in…?
- What are the steps you would take to do…?
- How would you organize your time and resources to start and complete a project on…?

Collaboration questions. You need to understand how a candidate would work with others in the organization. Outside of a one-person company, results are driven by multiple people or teams. The ability of someone to work well with others is critical. (By the way, this also extends to how successfully that person will be able to work with customers, partners, and vendors.) If you want a highly-functioning team and organization, a person can't just work well with you, the manager; he or she must be able to work well with peers too. Questions that screen for this:

- Ask candidates what they consider to be the primary principles / tenets in successfully working with other people in an organization.
- Ask them what traits or issues in other people stress them out / make it hard for them to work well.
- Have them give examples as to where they initially made mistakes or failed in working with others.

Management questions. Peer collaboration is a must for any position. Formal management responsibility is an entirely different matter. You need to have a huge level of trust in a potential manager, as his or her actions will have large consequences on the team and broader organization's strategy. Just as importantly (you can argue even more importantly), that manager will have a large impact on his or her staff: their contributions, growth and development, and livelihoods can or will depend on that manager and his or her ability. Spend the time to properly appraise these sorts of candidates. Core questions include:

- How do they organize their teams and resources to achieve the team / organizational goals?

- What are the traits they look for in candidates they hire themselves? Related, what is their hiring process? Experienced managers will have precise answers and views on hiring.

- Have them provide examples of how their management has contributed to the (professional) development of a subordinate / multiple subordinates.

- Have them explain their weaknesses as a supervisor, and importantly, what they have done or are doing to reduce those weaknesses. Look for specific answers, such as, "I've micro-managed too much in the past", or "I don't give enough positive acknowledgement to my team." Good leaders know their weaknesses.

- Provide examples on how they have failed a subordinate in managing expectations (professional, financial, etc.), supporting a subordinate's efforts, growing their skillset, etc. No manager is perfect.

- How do they assess people under their supervision and create plans for growth?

- How do they deal with a subordinate who isn't matching expectations? How long would they work on an improvement plan versus making a decision to find a replacement? This tells you much about their own ability to grow talent. The best managers can take almost any person and mold them into a good contributor given time, dedication, and resources. The converse side is that managers have to know when to retain someone on improvement plan versus finding a replacement.

Future goals and plans questions. This category is last and perhaps least important relative to all of the above. It is however worth understanding what a candidate wants to be doing in their career over the mid-term and long-term. Some may want the position only for the compensation and lack the fire / drive to apply 100% of themselves. Others might have a planned career path of going back to school or switching to a different type of role in the same field. It is less about impacting the organization in general (people are going to leave for many reasons over time), and more about helping you, the manager, evaluate that candidate's long-term potential. You might be fine with the candidate wanting to transition into a different type of role in two years because your organization has those sorts of alternate positions available. These questions provide good context.

Assessing Communication Skills

Throughout the entire interview, regardless of what type of question asked, pay attention to how candidates communicate. Start with the way they answer initial emails or during that first call, all the way through in-person interviews. Does every email you ever send have perfect grammar and diction? No, and communication doesn't require fancy words either. Attention to detail in the first times you communicate with someone is imperative, though. You get one shot with most potential employers and clients / customers. Sloppiness isn't a great selling point.

Beyond basic correctness, do they have the ability to convey their thoughts clearly? Again, not using fancy words or phrases, but clearly. Great communicators can make even complex topics accessible. The candidate may be communicating with your customers and vendors, and he or she will certainly communicate with other people in the organization. Both in one-on-one interviews, as well as any group interview, a sense should emerge about the candidate's communication skills. Sometimes it may be tricky to evaluate, for instance where natural nervousness in an interview setting paints a different picture. But discounting for the formal nature of most interviews, pay attention to the way in which he or she dialogues with you and other interviewers.

Culture Fit

Strong, well-defined organizational and team cultures help make the collective group greater than the sum of its parts. A strong culture makes people like their jobs more, and work longer / harder. Enough can't be said of a good culture. "Good" is a relative term. If it suits for the team or organization and makes them produce more and be happier than other environments or competitors, it can be a good culture. Good doesn't necessarily mean a fit for everyone though.

For the purposes of assessing candidates, you want (and need) to size up whether a candidate will fit inside of the bounds of the culture. You can do that through your own assessments of the person, as well as getting other team members' impressions from their individual or group interviews. It can well be that your team doesn't feel a candidate is a good fit and they are wrong. You may have more experience to see that the candidate is actually quite sociable, just shy, while your team feels that person won't fit in well because they are a loner. Ultimately, it is your decision as a manager, just pay attention to how well your decisions work out and evaluate how you can improve those decisions.

Know the chemistry of your culture, and be honest with yourself about whether a candidate will fit in. If your team is comprised mostly of twenty-something-year-old men and women who like to skateboard, the candidate is going to either be a twenty-something who likes to skateboard, or be a person that can associate with those types of people. You and that candidate must both understand the fit (or lack thereof) and decide on whether the culture feels right. Over time, you will have candidates (typically those with more experience who take the time to consider these things) pass on an offer, specifically citing their concerns about culture fit; it is great that they know themselves well enough to make such a decision.

Lastly, think not only of the current culture, but be bold and hire a candidate that will change the culture for the better.

Chapter 37: Making a Decision & Preparing an Offer

The time comes to make a decision on a candidate. If you hold yourself to just a few rules on making a hiring decision, let them be:

- Be highly passionate about someone you wish to hire, and let that passion be based on clear items you can identify and back up.
- Try to make each hire better than the last one.
- If you are hiring someone who will be a supervisor, ask yourself if you would work for the person if he or she was hiring you instead.

Don't attempt to fill a position in the short-term that lowers the ability of the team in the long-term. Raise the bar with every hire and you will achieve amazing results. Coupled with this, if you are not passionate about a hire, you aren't making the right decision. You should feel as if this is the best candidate for the position. That passion must be grounded in calm observation and analysis. If you are challenged on the candidate, do you have concrete points as to why you think he or she is the best fit? Or when challenged by your own boss or peer, do you quickly change your stance? If you do switch sides quickly, that means you haven't done your part thoroughly, either in your own evaluation or in the utilization of other experts to help you in the hiring decision.

Be transparent with all candidates in letting them know your hiring timelines. You can look to hire by a specific date, but you also might tell them that, while you want to fill the position as soon as possible, you will wait for the right person. Then, either way, give them a specific time frame by which they will hear from you, with good news or not. For positions with a lot of applicant volume, a good method is to let them know that you make decisions on a weekly basis on whether a candidate has received a position, is still in consideration, or is no longer being considered.

Avoid stringing candidates along for unknown periods of time. The best candidates will take other offers, and all candidates dislike the idea of floating without knowing whether they are going to get an offer or not. You don't want to make hasty hires, but you also don't want to hesitate on the trigger with a great candidate on the off-chance someone potentially better applies the next day.

With candidates that don't make the cut in any stage of the process, you have the option of providing them feedback as to why. Some could not care less to speak with you, others are curious and wish to improve. It is your discretion as to how much you share. The smoothest approach is to supply feedback to only candidates who ask for it, and then be honest and give them concrete ways to improve for other opportunities.

What about for someone who is overqualified for the position? One of the hardest calls I've had to make was on a position where I had someone who was truly talented, but over-qualified for the position, which was a junior level placement. I knew that three months after hiring that person, she would be on par with people making a lot more money and become unhappy, and my budget for the position was completely fixed. I would have short-term gains but a long-term loss. So, I spent fifteen minutes on the phone explaining, in detail, that she should apply to other more senior positions, and some hints as to how to improve the initial resume. It was a win-win situation. A month later, the person contacted me saying that she had found a job much more in line with her ability, while I ended up making an offer to a separate candidate perfect for my particular position. This is the risk you run in ever hiring someone who is over-qualified. At some point, he or she will become dissatisfied if you, as the manager, cannot give him or her more compensation and / or more opportunities.

When you have found the right candidate, make the offer. There is sometimes a fear of making a decision because the manager wishes to wait for a few more resumes, as if some magical person will appear. That rarely happens. If you follow the rules of choosing carefully and being passionate about a hire, you will do well.

Structuring an Offer

When you make a decision, waste no time in putting an offer together. If you have done a good job of explaining the role and the opportunity, you will get a positive response back the majority of the time.

Don't expect your offer to always be accepted on the spot. Some applicants may do that, others will counter immediately, and yet others will ask for some time to consider the offer (often to talk it over with a significant other or others). All are acceptable scenarios you should allow for. The big variable in hiring offers almost always comes down to financial compensation. You offer X, and the candidate comes back by saying, "I want X + 10%." Sometimes it is realistic, sometimes not.

One method is asking a candidate for their desired salary range. A manager may have a range for a position from $37,000 to a maximum of $43,000, and the candidate says his or her range is $35,000 to $40,000. Some managers (shortsightedly) ask for ranges as a way to figure out the minimum amount of dollars a candidate will accept for the position. That can backfire, especially as many candidates know this little "trick" and will balk at you coming back with an offer at the low end of their range. If you have the dollars, you should be looking for and want to compensate a candidate that deserves what you can pay.

You can also choose to have the entire compensation discussion during the interview process, where you tell them what the position pays, either an exact figure or a small range. If it is an exact figure, it is assumed to be - and you should make it clear - the maximum amount you can pay. If it is a range, a candidate will immediately ask for the maximum amount, unless you make clear that the highest figure is for candidates with more experience or some other key qualification. But again, you want a candidate worth their salary.

The probable best method combines both exact figures and ranges. Ask for a range, and if their compensation is in the general maximum amount you are willing to pay, be transparent and let them know the figure. If their range or amount is greater than your maximum, you should either let them know it is a deal-breaker and still offer them your maximum and see if they are amenable to that, given any other benefits of the position, or you can go to your own supervisor / boss and make the case for the additional money.

Now, if you constantly have to go to your boss and argue that a good candidate needs more than your previously established maximum, you are doing something wrong and it won't reflect well on you; you haven't done your compensation research well enough, you are finding people more senior than expected, or you are not managing expectations properly. But every once in a while there is a special candidate where you may feel compelled to make a case. Make it a good one and you may get the funds. That is a judgement call on the candidate and your perceived likelihood about getting more money for that position.

The candidate always has an option of countering with another figure. By having had the conversation(s) before the formal offer, you will limit these sorts of counters. At the end of the day, if you haven't exhausted the maximum possible you can offer or you make the case to the organization and get an additional allotment, you can always decide to agree to a counter or meet the candidate part-way.

When an Offer is Declined

It will happen to you. The best candidates usually have numerous opportunities. Sometimes it means negotiating with the candidate; sometimes the sides simply can't align; sometimes the candidate doesn't feel it is the best fit; many possible reasons. When this transpires, avoid a common pitfall of blindly trying to hire the second-best candidate. If the margin between the two (or three or four) top candidates was narrow and you have a pack of great people, go ahead. Often though, second-best candidates are a long way from being as good as the first, and it comes down more to a manager not wanting to keep the search process active and the position open. If the second choice is amazing, make the offer; if not, resist the urge to pull the trigger and keep looking. Stay true to your hiring goals.

Chapter 38: Reference Checks

There is one important step to make either immediately before the formal offer, or to make an offer contingent on: reference checks. Don't confuse these with simple verifications of employment history. Reference checks are more in-depth communications about a candidate to confirm all of the things he or she has told you about, as well as to find out any issues he or she hasn't told you about or may not be as aware of.

Generally, candidates don't like potential employers to contact references unless they are in the last stages of consideration for a position. That's a fair request, given that references are busy people in and of themselves, and don't want to be bothered by every potential organization to which someone applies. Reference checks of this sort take some time on the potential employer's part as well, so many tend to structure it so that an offer letter is valid contingent on reference checks as well as a background check.

Don't underestimate the value of properly constructed reference checks. The secret, of course, is knowing how to construct them.

How many references you should request? Most employers ask for two or three references as the standard, with no specifics as to the type of reference provided. Almost anyone can provide two people who will speak well of them. Going more in depth yields more interesting results. For anyone even just two years out of college, ask for four references. Specifically, two mentors or seniors, and two peer references. Add one reference of each type for each additional one to two years of experience. If the candidate has managerial experience or is applying for a position with supervisory duties, also ask for references of subordinates (people he or she has managed).

It is worth telling the origin story of how I first heard about the importance of reference checks. During one of the first conferences I ever attended, when I was nineteen years old, I listened to the founder of a large private equity firm talk about his victories. He said good hires were a key component of his success, and that he mandated that applicants for CEO positions in his portfolio companies submit twenty references. Anyone at a CEO level could submit five or ten names, he said, but it gets real interesting when you get to twenty. It is much harder to produce twenty curated names. You get to people who will actually tell you the good and the bad.

Building on this, given that interaction with peers and a team is so critical, talking with multiple types of references make sense. And why not speak with the people a supposedly good manager has supervised? If he or she has done a consistently good job over time, there shouldn't be a problem producing names.

Reference checks are especially vital to applicants with more experience, such as senior managers. It is depressingly common that, six months after a senior manager is hired, his or her team culture stinks, and the team is nowhere near their full potential. Digging in, you find that proper diligence was never done on their past management skills and achievements during the hiring period. Great, they supposedly grew their teams' revenue by 20%, or increased efficiency by 30%. Seemingly impressive numbers can be thrown around that are ultimately not a direct result of that person's management. The overall organization may have launched an amazing marketing campaign, or it may have been the top "lieutenants" of that manager who were the real secret behind the success. Many elements can create a good result, and it takes proper diligence to fully know if that manager caused the positive result himself or herself, or if he or she simply benefited from broader positive trends.

The two primary purposes of conducting a reference check are to confirm that a candidate has been truthful in stating their strengths and accomplishments, as well as to get a third party's insight into any weaknesses the candidate might have (that they either didn't disclose or are unaware of).

Here are some core questions to ask references:

- In what capacity did you work with the candidate and for how long?

- What was the candidate's most impressive accomplishment during the time you worked with him or her?

- Confirm certain key accomplishments or figures stated by the candidate.

- Did the candidate communicate and explain things clearly?

- How did he or she work with peers, with supervisors, or with his or her direct reports?

- What were some of the ways you saw the candidate develop or grow over time?

- Give an example of a scenario where the candidate failed or responded poorly, and how he or she improved afterwards.

- What do you think the candidate's areas or opportunities for improvement were or are?

Come up with additional questions based on the specific role and the things you feel are important to know. Don't underestimate the value of speaking with people who have known a candidate for a long time.

It is a happy moment when you make an offer to a great candidate, he or she accepts that offer, and everything falls into place. The first day that person starts work for you and with your team is a day of energy and new opportunity.

Chapter 39: Environment & Culture

The environment and culture that you create for your team greatly impacts their productivity and happiness. It decides what type of people work in the organization; who applies, who stays, and who goes. It defines the way those people act, think, and their self-accountability. Organizational culture can be hard to define. It simultaneously encompasses the way each member feels about the team and broader organization, as well as the ways in which they feel comfortable communicating and expressing themselves.

If there are only two questions to ask about the status of an organization's culture, they may be:

- Do its members want to come into work?
- Do members feel that there is a supportive and opportunity-filled environment?

Ask yourself if your culture meets the above two criteria, and if not, why.

No single type of culture is perfect or right for every organization, though every good organization should have a strong culture if it wants to attract talented people and achieve its goals. The job of a proactive manager is to help and craft a positive culture that fits his or her organization. Culture doesn't exist only at the organizational level; individual divisions, even individual teams, can foster radically different cultures within the same organization.

Many elements affect culture, including:

- Management philosophy of the senior leadership
- Industry

- Core goals of the organization
- Historical approach to the organization's culture
- Size of the organization
- Average age / generation of the people in the organization
- Physical proximity of the organization's members to one another (Are people all in one location or in multiple locations?)
- Formality and methods of communication between peers, as well as between a team and its manager
- Layout and design of the office
- Ability of division / team managers to augment the overall organizational culture
- ...and therefore the management philosophy of the division / team leaders

As with the number of different social groups in the world, there are many different types of organizational cultures that keep people happy and motivated. To be clear, you can and should construct a highly inclusive culture. The best cultures don't have boundaries on things like age, social status, or weekend hobbies. The people on the team are open-minded and focused on getting their work done well in a supportive environment. They may never spend time with one another outside of the office setting and that is fine.

The larger the team or organization, the more developed and self-sustaining the culture becomes. It creates an atmosphere and dynamic which can immediately attract or repel job candidates, even if the existing team is very happy.

As a manager, you have to first square your own feelings – good or bad - about an organization's culture, and then figure out how much impact you can have on shaping that culture. If you are given a lot of latitude and autonomy to run your team, you can shape a distinctive culture, although, as a warning, if that culture makes your team feel like the rest of the organization is far worse or poor, you will cause larger rifts and divides. Shape the culture as much as you can, but ensure it fits into the culture of the rest of the organization. Like with team strategy driving organizational strategy, your team culture should positively complement the organizational culture.

Within those bounds, you have much opportunity to create a

culture that helps you achieve your goals. Focus on:

- Defining the values of the team. Moral values, of course, but also by defining what traits and characteristics in people are most valued. For instance, do you emphasize a completely quantitative approach to arguments and presentations, or qualitative? How competitive do you want your team to be, or is it less about competitiveness and more about organic idea creation? There are thousands of different blends.
- Relating the values to the primary strategic initiatives of the team and the organization.
- Identifying and highlighting the people on the team that best showcase the values you wish everyone to maintain.
- Creating fun, engaging activities and rituals in the team that mesh people together.
- Ensuring that the team culture complements the organizational culture, to eliminate negative feelings and foster positive collaboration.

You should really take pleasure in creating a culture. Have your senior team members aid in parts of it, champion it, and use it to bind the team together to drive robust results.

Chapter 40: Firing & Replacing Team Members

The heaviest responsibility that a manager has is the duty of firing someone.

Firing someone is firing someone. You can sugarcoat the term and call it "termination", or "replacement", or "letting someone go," but that simply glosses over the reality - and it shouldn't be glossed over - that firing someone creates a massive impact on his or her professional as well as personal life. You should never like to fire.

Three of the most common reasons for which people are fired:

1) They commit an immediately fireable offense themselves, such as theft, aggression against co-workers, etc.

2) The organization decides to reduce its staff by decision of senior managers and / or macro forces like bad economic times or other factors that affect the prospects of an organization.

3) They don't commit an immediately fireable offense, but have enough smaller infractions or issues with the organization that a decision is made to fire them.

The first scenario doesn't require much explanation. It is unfortunate that someone chooses to take that sort of negative action, but if the facts and evidence are clear, you must fire him or her and move on.

The second scenario is the worst because it can impact good employees and contributors. Junior and mid-level managers particularly get the short end of the stick, as they are often given this type of news after the fact and are left to make decisions about who they must let go. At times, it can mean letting more than one person go at the same time. Remember that you should make the announcement to everyone impacted at the same time. Be as clear and transparent as possible as to why this is happening. Ensure that the team members not impacted know they are not impacted, and don't do multiple rounds of firing. Nothing kills team morale and the desire to contribute like uncertainty about your livelihood. Let everyone know as soon as possible, to give them the maximum possible time to start looking for other jobs. Where cases warrant it and you have the ability, you can work in severance packages.

Firing Based on Your Decision

The third scenario is the most common and requires the most explanation and decision-making. It is the one that is more of your decision as to how and when to do it versus the other two. These are the cases where you have team members who are not working out, for a number of reasons, including:

- Underperformance or poor performance over time, relative to stated expectations.
- Repeat or succession of offenses that, while not immediately fireable offenses, create a negative pattern.
- Constant friction with other team members, customers, or vendors.

You should never like firing but, in these cases, you must understand that it is a necessary tool and action to be used.

Here is what many managers fail to realize: A bad employee doesn't just hurt him or herself, or make your life miserable. He or she makes the entire team's life miserable. Your great employees wonder why that person is still on the team, as they will be keen on everyone pulling their own weight. Meanwhile, your middle-of-the-range employees use it to justify their own excuses, problems, or laziness.

At the end of the day, your team and the organization is bigger than you or the person who must be let go. It's very easy to forget that. In smaller teams, one person not performing well, let alone performing poorly, weighs everyone down.

Don't treat the act of firing casually, and make every attempt to fix the situation by other means first. No one is perfect at all times. We all make mistakes or have personal issues that affect performance in the workplace at one point or another. The decision for you to make as a manager is whether these issues are temporary or can be fixed. Fixing the situation does not mean ignoring or sitting on it though. Create clear boundaries and limits and follow them.

When you have attempted everything in your power, tried every conceivable solution or alternative, and nothing has fixed the situation, then action must be taken. One note of warning: Don't ever let anyone on your team overly influence this decision. It is yours to make, not theirs, and that must be made clear. Listen to and document verified evidence, but decisions should not be made on hearsay, but rather on clear and evident patterns.

In any team larger than a few people, you will never have a team of "A" level players in perpetuity. It can and should certainly be a goal, but typically, at best, you have a series of "A" players, and a smaller group of "B" players that you believe have the potential to become "A" players with your support. Remember, too, that everything is relative. If you have truly established a great team overall, every person may in fact be an "A" player when compared to other teams and organizations. But within your team, there will still be some people who are better contributors and performers than others.

If your goal is to have a fantastic team, you need fantastic people on that team to achieve fantastic results. (Note the use of the word "fantastic" three times.) Therefore, every person on your team is either:

- A fantastic employee you want to keep.
- An average employee you are training and developing into a fantastic employee.
- A poor employee who you are *in the process of replacing.*

The words "in the process of replacing" are very deliberate. The reality is that you can't always fire someone on the exact day you want to fire him or her. He or she may either hold a role that would cripple the deliverables and timetables you have set or that have been set upon you if his or her position suddenly becomes vacant, or it may place large burdens on your remaining team members. Obviously, if he or she commits an offense that requires immediate termination, or you are told to fire him or her by a senior manager, you have no choice.

A proactive manager anticipates these types of circumstances, instead of simply reacting to them after the fact. That manager, upon realizing they have an employee who must be fired, either:

1) Terminates that person after planning to re-allocate the workload among other parts of the team. (In certain circumstances, you can share news with and plan ahead with team members; in others, for legal & liability purposes, you must make the termination without letting other employees know beforehand. All of these are specific situations that should be discussed with your HR department.)

2) Begins the hiring / recruitment process to fill the position and proceeds with the termination only when a new team member has been identified and committed to the soon-vacant position, to ensure continuity. (These are often issued as confidential job postings.)

You must separate personal feelings from the necessity of keeping continuity. You can seek to ease the transition process for the person being terminated. Whether you have the power to offer certain considerations or need to work with your HR department / supervisor, there are numerous options: severance, continued insurance coverage, or helping him or her find a new position by offering third-party placement or services.

When you have made the decision to fire someone and have done what is necessary to safeguard the team and its direction, fire fast. Get it over with and move on to the more positive duties of your position.

Chapter 41: External Experts & Resources

While non-managers (including sales teams) sometimes get to work with clients or vendors, most of the time it is in a limited capacity of producing work for the client or in taking care of daily operational requirements. The big decisions - strategy development and negotiations - are taken care of by managers. The problem here for new managers: not much, if any, experience with how to deal with these types of matters. That inexperience results in avoidable mistakes which cost time and money.

Using External Resources & Experts

Previous sections in the book covered the importance of understanding your team's strengths and weaknesses, and its abilities as compared to other organizations and resources. Even the largest of organizations have deficits in certain types of knowledge or expertise. What areas you choose to develop internally versus leverage outside resources for is an important decision. That decision should always tie back to your team's and organization's strategy. If it is an area that is critical to the execution of the strategy, you should ensure that your team can carry out the duty.

A common example would be a small-business not being able to afford an experienced CFO full-time to help with long-term financial objectives and therefore relying instead on a part-time financial consultant. Another example would be a firm wanting to shoot a television commercial they know won't be reshot very often and deciding to use a thirty-party organization for the video production. In both cases, when you have decided that you currently don't have or don't want to invest in building a certain type of expertise in-house, the use of external resources - vendors and partners - becomes necessary. Don't think of using external resources only for the major tasks or projects that require attention, but also for highly specialized smaller tasks or decisions that benefit from true expertise.

When it is to be a single person acting as a consultant, vet them in the same ways you would a potential full-time team member.

If you are hiring multiple people or a third-party organization as an external resource, make sure to do conduct thorough evaluations as well. The reason to stress this is that new managers often commit two mistakes here. First, they don't see the importance of outside resources because they haven't used them directly very much in the past. Second, when they do decide to use external resources, they don't employ a good method of assessing those resources.

You should think of every potential external relationship in the same vein as a potential new employee, in the way that you carefully assess their abilities to produce results and evaluate the costs involved. Part of this includes using trusted experts to make a determination of an external resource's ability before you make the commitment. Like any candidate applying for a job, no vendor or partner ever says, "Hire me because I'm average or second-rate." Everyone calls themselves great, and it takes an expert in the space to truly gauge that. If this seems obvious to you, congratulations. But perhaps because of ego (thinking they know better) or time (not wanting to wait longer to do a proper evaluation), many managers fail to assess third parties properly. This frequently results in a task taking longer to accomplish than expected, costing much more, or never being completed at all.

For instance, take a business owner or manager who decides that their organization should have a new website. The expertise to do so isn't found in-house, so they decide to hire a third-party developer or development firm to build the website. The research process lasts only an hour or two and unearths either the largest or the closest possible vendors. How much they are willing to spend is often an arbitrary number as that manager doesn't really know what it should cost; or worse, they allow the development firm they have contacted to tell them what it should cost, with no idea of whether that figure is accurate or not. Project specifications are not completed ahead of time, but rather are worked through on the first call with the potential vendor. The decision on which external resource to go with often relies solely on price and is only between two or three options. This is akin to putting a job posting out, speaking with only the first three candidates that apply for the position, and hiring the first one that says they will do a good job after speaking with them on the phone.

It is not that all vendors and partners are out to fleece you; most are very honest and hard-working. But inexperienced managers somehow have a special talent for finding the dishonest or incompetent vendor. To evaluate external resources properly:

1) Assemble all possible requirements for the task or project that necessitate an outside resource.
2) Use trusted expert resources to help you assess needs and costs - your organization, your network, a different existing trusted vendor, qualified review websites - someone should know something.
3) Create a proposal that lists all requirements.
4) Send the proposal out to at least five vendors, if at all possible.
5) Eliminate any vendors that come back with initial bids too far outside of your cost and time parameters.
6) Hold initial discussions with each party to allow them to better understand your needs and for you to learn more about them.
7) Vet the remaining vendors by seeing examples of recent work and speaking with existing clients. (No good vendor has a problem with providing client references.)
8) In certain cases, ask for a second or final round of bids / quotes on the proposed project.
9) Negotiate the cost and time required, as well as other factors / deliverables that you wish to be part of the project.

Once you do establish close relationships with a set of trusted experts, these are the people you can turn to again and again for advice on work or projects that you need assistance with. Just like you build a strong internal team, build a network of external resources. These people pay for themselves many times over.

Conclusion

This section has explored every major area of finding the right people for your team, and ensuring those people are of the proper quality. It is the longest section in the book because so much hinges on the people who assist you in fulfilling your team's and organization's mission. Spend as much time as possible creating strong hiring processes and constructing an environment that stellar contributors will want to be a part of. If you can master the ability to regularly make strong hires, you will be able to scale your results across the organization and rise quickly in your career.

Section Five: Growing Your Team

As a manager, you need to ensure your team accomplishes the strategic initiatives that you and / or the organization have planned. You build a powerhouse team not only by making good hires, but also through growing the talent you have internally. "Growing" means working with them to raise their technical / operational skills in the areas required, as well as their soft skills and their ability to contribute to smart tactics and strategies that help you reach your goals.

New managers (new to management and those in new positions) often drive hard in the first couple of months to build their team to a level that allows them to meet their strategic objectives. That is, of course, critical. At this point though, many managers stop driving. They feel as if their current team can get to the finish line with enough pushing and prodding on the manager's behalf, and they become satisfied with the status quo. How much upside those types of managers lose; the heights to which they could have gotten if they continued to unlock a team's full potential.

It takes a few months, on average, for a new team member to get familiar with a team and an organization's processes, understand its goals, bond with their co-workers, and really harness the full potential that they can bring to the table. A good manager can often - but certainly not always - gauge that full potential before his or her new employee does, but it takes time to evaluate if the person is going to meet expectations, let alone blow them away as he or she gets up to speed.

As a good manager, as soon as you have the team executing the work necessary to meet its goals, you should be building talent; the skills and abilities that will help you succeed as well as take your people to great heights in their careers. This is a wonderfully self-reinforcing cycle. As you develop the talent on your team, you, in turn, can achieve more. The more you achieve, the more opportunities and resources you are given, which you can then again develop. This cycle continues on and on.

Chapter 42: Your Approach & Expectations as the Manager

Every decision and action you take is scrutinized and weighed much more heavily when you become a manager. You may not realize it initially, but that is truly the case. It isn't as much increased scrutiny from your supervisor, but from your team. As a mentor, leader, and champion of / for a group of people, you have a large responsibility for them and influence on them.

Even a small comment on a subject can propel the entire team to take a stance. If you lack concern about a certain detail, the team likely won't care. A decision that you make in regards to the way someone acts - well or badly - is digested by the entire team and used as context for their own actions.

Every move you make should be weighed in the scope of how it will affect one or all of the people on your team. Know that you set the example. You never have to be perfect and you certainly shouldn't act as if you are. Be human, make mistakes sometimes, and acknowledge that others will make mistakes. But work hard, work smart, and establish good patterns of communication, and you will create a solid foundation for success. The following principles build on the approaches to success from Part One, with a few further nuances for managers.

Humbleness & Giving Credit

Managers - young managers especially (and almost by definition) - are an over-confident bunch. A bit of humbleness will take you a long way. You should still sell yourself, but you must realize that selling yourself as a manager means going away from the use of the word "I" and moving to the use of the word "we."

You can be a genius, but if your team performs poorly and you miss achieving your required goals, you are to blame. You can't throw your team to the wolves; they are your responsibility and a reflection on you.

By the same proxy, when you achieve something great, give credit to the team member(s) responsible. If you have insightful bosses who understand your role in driving the strategy and running your team, they will know you created the environment for that success. You look better for not taking personal credit explicitly and instead receive it implicitly.

A common sign of a bad to average manager is the way in which he or she talks about his or her professional accomplishments. Great managers have two things going for them. They have a wonderful team that helps them be successful, and they have a reputation built upon that fact, because everyone knows their accomplishments weren't achieved alone. If you come across a manager (especially of larger teams) who constantly says "I did this" and "I did that" versus "the team accomplished this," you are likely dealing with an insecure manager who is not a good builder of talent to boot. Sure, he or she may be a great contributor, but in any organization, down to a small start-up, it is the efforts of many people, coupled and enhanced by a great manager, that make for great results. Understand that fact, be humble, and appreciate your team.

It seems like a small change to be more humble, using "we" instead of "I," and giving your team the credit, but it will help to set up your reputation as a good leader.

Communication & Managing Expectations

Managers typically operate at a fast pace. In the midst of that pace, mistakes and issues are often still caught, but positive momentum and communication frequently get taken for granted.

The smallest, easiest thing a manager can do is to verbally acknowledge the great things an individual or group have accomplished. This tiny, quick thing is often overlooked. What ends up happening is that a manager realizes he or she has left it too long and makes a belated (usually larger) show of appreciation that everyone knows is a bit hollow. Thanks and congratulations during and immediately after the fact work much better. On the other side of the coin, if you show your appreciation even when failures occur, you dilute the value of the positive reinforcement. It is always a balance.

Beyond personal praise, remember the value of communicating to your team and managing expectations like they are adults, consistently sharing information. Adults of any age dislike being talked down to or feeling like they aren't told something because the manager(s) thinks they can't handle it. There may be certain things a manager can't tell his or her employees, such as a pending acquisition that is confidential. But far and wide, managers fail to tell teams even the essentials, sometimes because they feel the team couldn't handle or digest the information well or would get distracted, and sometimes because they (wrongly) assume the team already knows the information.

Even in a smaller team, you might be surprised by how many won't know the full strategy because they are focused on their own particular part of it. It is your responsibility as a manager to increase their awareness. Invest your team into the strategy and organization and make them want to work like owners of the organization! It will make such a tremendous difference. Not only will your team feel more empowered, but the energy and idea generation across multiple types of specialties and personalities will lead to truly magical things.

Your Relationship to Your Team

While there are many different types of management styles, there are certain bounds that you shouldn't cross. As a peer with someone, you can talk casually with them about any subject, confer on what you think about others and how to affect change, and create true friends.

If you cross those bounds or allow them to be crossed as a manager, you lose influence and authority over your team. You can immensely enjoy the kinship of your team, but as long as you are someone's supervisor, you can be a mentor and a leader, but never a friend. You should retain the ability to make decisions objectively about people and their performance. Not only do you cloud your own judgement when you get too close with someone you supervise, but you also diminish your credibility with other members of your team, who will suspect, if not outright accuse you of, favoritism.

If a manager engages in any sort of favoritism, it should be based on strong performance and standards anyone in the team can achieve if they try hard enough, not based simply on the years a person has known the manager, shared hobbies, or flattery. Don't forget the good things someone on your team has done in times past, but if that person coasts on past performance and not on present, you will, knowingly or not, diminish the potential of the entire team.

This sort of separation isn't easy. Not at all. Almost no one is an emotionless automaton. Many managers do choose to become friends with their subordinates, and those who don't, often want to. You will make your own decisions on this subject, like the others in this book, and figure out an approach that works best for you and your management style.

Empathy

While you need to keep professional distance, as a manager the need for empathy only grows. You can't create a team of clones of yourself. You can try, but at best you will gain a set of "yes" men and "yes" women who think exactly like you do and can't offer different perspectives or approaches. There is great value in having a mix of people, and the reality is that you will almost always have a very diverse set of people on your team.

Too regularly, managers fail to empathize with others who don't fit in the same mold. They can't seem to grasp that Ronald the administrative assistant loves his job. He has been doing it for 30 years, knows it inside and out, is good at it, and he is, quite simply, happy. That Ronald isn't an executive at his age, or that he clocks at out 5:00pm to go dancing with his wife or work on the garden boggles the mind of a someone focused on making as much money and building as much success as fast as possible. "Ronald is unambitious," they think. Or, "He must not be that smart." Sure, some Ronalds in the world don't have what it takes on the professional or social level to keep climbing the ranks; some destroy their trajectories with poor decisions or actions. But many simply have different priorities that they have decided on or accepted. That doesn't mean that they can't be excellent contributors and members of the team. You will never have a team or organization of any size that is only composed of one type of person.

If you don't understand what truly drives someone to perform at their best, based on their personal values, professional expectations, and goals, how can you maximize their performance? You have to truly learn about each of the people on your team. You will often be surprised by the various skills, traits, and talents that someone may have, and it is simply a too-specific set of duties that has been the limiting factor.

How Can I Help You? (On Steroids)

The mantra of "How can I help you?" applies to many more situations for you as a manager, and you gain many more resources to implement that help.

You can apply this approach with other teams, managers, and external parties such as customers and vendors, now harnessing the various people and materials at your disposal to create solutions. This sort of approach builds your team's reputation as a strong and dependable resource.

You also now need to use the "How can I help you?" approach with your individual team, in the way you coach them and develop them in their careers and skills. It really is an open secret that the more you give, the more you get.

Understand your people, communicate well with them, manage their expectations, and you will create a powerful environment for success.

Chapter 43: Evaluations & Assessments

An earlier chapter in Part Two focused on the initial evaluations you conduct when you first become a manager. These initial appraisals are not uncommon. Where we stumble is ensuring that evaluations for each and every team member are ongoing and consistent. That is a sure way by which to continuously grow the skills and contribution potential of each person on your team.

The Passion Index

Here is an exercise for you:

1) Write down a list of all of your team members' names.
2) Close your eyes and point to a name on that list.
3) Open your eyes and see which name your finger rests on.
4) What is the first thought that comes to mind when you think about that person?

Now, let's break it down. Was that first thought or memory something positive about what he or she did for the team or organization, or something negative? Put more simply, did you initially smile or frown?

This "Passion Index" can assist you in categorizing your true feelings on the performance of one of your team members. Day to day, everyone has ups and downs. As a good manager, you have to understand and accept that no one is perfect; we all have better days and worse days. Over time, however, you do build an image of that team member based on his or her actions and performance. These patterns are useful in helping to make informed decisions. Now of course, don't fire people because you frown when you think of them. But, as you regularly sit down and evaluate your team, the Passion Index is indicative of how well a team member is performing to your expectations. How many are you truly passionate about keeping on your team?

A good part of that relies on you crafting expectations and making those expectations clear to a particular team member, as well as to yourself. Those expectations must be realistic, or you set yourself and the team member up for failure. It is important to remember that every person has their own set of priorities. Bob might know he can make 15% more at another organization, but he would have to work an additional ten hours a week and Bob wants that time to spend with his young children. Judy really only loves one part of her job and does excellent work there, while other elements suffer.

The big picture is pretty binary: A team member's performance must constantly come in above the lower bound a manager has established. A person can always outperform your expectations, but not continuously perform worse. An earlier chapter discussed the unfortunate reality of having to fire someone from your team, but this chapter focuses on how to do everything in your power to keep that from happening. Almost anyone can succeed professionally, if they have the personal drive to succeed (their responsibility) and are given proper mentorship and goals they can achieve (your responsibility).

Reviews & Planning

In many organizations, everything revolves around what is called the "annual performance review." Once a year, a manager sits down with each of his or her team members and speaks to them about their achievements and strengths, their weaknesses, and any changes in position (promotions) and compensation that are available to them. This is a horribly rigid system for performance evaluation, especially because many managers tend to save up - or simply not think about - a team member's performance or improvement opportunities until that annual review.

Case example: One member of your team, Sam, has consistently (for the past three months) been sending reports to clients that contain one or two small errors. No horrible mistakes, but the errors are constant, and you know they should be caught. As you review the document, you make the changes every time and mention it once to Sam in a casual conversation. During Sam's next annual review, you suddenly tell him you are fed up with the avoidable errors. Sam is surprised when you bring it up.

Is Sam just pretending that he doesn't know what is going on, or did you do something wrong? Which one do you think? Answer: What you (didn't) do is worse than what Sam did.

During a formal review, if you mention something that has been bothering you and / or affecting your team member's performance, *and it honestly surprises the person when you bring it up,* you haven't held up your end of the relationship. To be blunt, this is bad management on your part.

The point of a formal review is not to bring up small issues. What, then, is the purpose? You should be doing all of the following in the review:

- Discuss how the team member has improved his or her skills or performance since the last review or since joining the team.
- Establish the areas in which that person can continue to improve, through his or her own learning and ways in which you can support his or her growth.
- Create the long-term plan for the next six or twelve months on what the team member wants to achieve and what you want them to achieve; new skillsets, more leadership opportunities, different responsibilities, promotions, etc.
- Promote the team member and / or give him or her more compensation. This last point depends on how your organization approaches this matter. Many organizations only allow for promotions or changes in compensation during an annual review or in special cases where large changes in responsibility occur.

These formal reviews go into deep discussions on the future direction and desires of your team member in greater detail than you normally do. If the review takes you only ten minutes, you have likely missed the point.

Notice how the above list failed to mention incremental feedback from the team member to you, or your incremental feedback to the team member. Both directions of that communication should be constant and never wait for reviews.

Because time flies and everyone gets busy, it is wise to specifically carve out times to regularly speak with team members as a check-in. Beyond the annual review, sit down at least every three months with each person on your team for an in-depth conversation. If this seems like a lot, remember that your ability to recognize their needs and increase their potential - not you doing work yourself - is what leads to the big successes as a manager. Invest in people. Keep the following in mind:

- Constantly think about how you can help team members do better by allowing them to learn other areas from their co-workers, through your direct mentorship, or by subsidizing continuing education.
- Constantly think about the future of each team member in relation to what you can provide. What do your team members want to achieve professionally? Do you have those opportunities available for them when they are ready? What can you do to help them be ready for when those opportunities present themselves?

Incremental Feedback

You should encourage and practice an atmosphere of constant feedback. Use the three-month meetings to ensure that all concerns and opportunities are being addressed. Otherwise, act in real time. In the earlier example with Sam, he should have been made more immediately aware of his errors, especially after the second time. Just as praise should be incremental, so should feedback on errors and opportunities for improvement.

Consider the following:

- When an issue occurs, provide feedback immediately to the person.
- Explain the issue and why it is an issue (what you think is a problem may not be apparent to the team member).
- Discuss why it happened. Mistakes often happen from a lack of knowledge or understanding, and those types of mistakes are your responsibility as a manager. Teach that person the correct way, have someone else teach them, or assign the task / responsibility to someone else.
- Explain how you can keep it from happening again, if it is a one-off mistake. Be patient and supportive the first time

an issue occurs, unless it was caused by laziness or negligence. Ensure the team member feels accountable if the task remains part of his or her responsibility.

- For issues that will require time to fix or education on how to not make them in the future, establish clear deadlines by which that person should have it resolved or re-learned.

- If the same mistake occurs again, even if it is a minor one, be firmer with the person, as you made him or her accountable. Discuss what repercussions will happen if it occurs a third time. Think about whether you should require him or her to learn a process again or assign it to someone else. If you decide that the team member will remain responsible for the task, keep holding him or her accountable and checking in on the progress.

It comes down to the frequency of those mistakes and what steps that person takes to keep them from happening again. To be very clear, the above deals with issues outside of the bounds of planned mistakes and new learning. You should never come down hard on a team member who is still familiarizing him or herself with a new process, or testing new initiatives within the bounds you have previously set. If you do, you squash innovation and a desire to push boundaries, as your team will be fearful to try new things. That will cripple you.

Chapter 44: Delegation

The concept of "delegation" may be one of the more common hurdles in the transition from contributor to manager. Most contributors become managers initially on the basis of having performed superlative work. They either did all of the work themselves, or worked with a team where they still had a hand in almost every part of the tasks or projects that were completed successfully.

Life changes when you become a manager. Even as a manager of just one person, you start to realize (sometimes sooner, sometimes later) that you can't do everything yourself. You try to keep up, pulling long hours, insisting that everything pass your scrutiny before it goes out. Then you either burn out or you learn a smarter way.

That smarter way involves trust. It requires an ability to accept small mistakes. It is delegation.

Delegation frees you up to focus on the bigger strategy picture, dive into particular areas that need your specialized or managerial attention, and build the skills of your team.

On the subject of strategy, delegation is not about passing off the boring or non-fun work to others, but it is your responsibility to manage your time well to be most effective. Ask yourself what you can be doing and then what you should be doing with your time. The two areas that are most important as a manager - strategy and team building - should receive priority over other work that one of your team members can accomplish. Both areas require time, perspective, and energy. You can try to do them while doing twenty other things, but you will suffer for it.

When you are not focused on the two key areas, you still need to keep blocks of time open for whatever issues or needs arise during the day. It is never about being too good to do any type of work; there will be times where you assist in the most basic of work that needs doing simply because it is your job to get the team to the finish line. Basic work or not however, there are constantly going to be areas that need your attention or expertise. If you are stuck doing another piece of work that could have been done by a member of your team, you end up either dropping one item to work on the other, or working until midnight. There is not anything wrong with working long hours; we all have to during certain periods when things are very busy, but you will burn yourself out with that sort of approach. More importantly, the two areas that almost always suffer during these periods are your ability to develop strategy and build your team.

Delegation vs. Micromanaging

Here are a few questions to ask yourself to see how well you delegate:

When you are not around, does your team function (well) without you? Are you the bottleneck in your team? Is the team so used to asking your advice on problems or strategy that a freeze occurs in your absence? If your answer is anything short of, "my team does a kick-butt job even when I'm not around," you have work to do. Instead of delegating, you are actually micro-managing. You may think you are giving work to others, but you still end up reviewing everything before it goes out (to customers, partners, other teams, bosses, etc.). Ask yourself what you need to do versus what you just like doing or don't trust your team to do. If it is a question of trust, realize that that is a problem which you will need to solve by either training your team better or hiring the right resources to do the job well. That is a key function of scaling and growing.

To effectively delegate, the following are important points to remember:

- Treat time as the most precious commodity you have, and use it carefully.
- Prioritize the importance of tasks and projects.
- Figure out which tasks can be done completely by someone else, which ones require supervision or review, and which can be done only by you.

- Assign out all tasks that don't require your involvement to complete.
- Review those tasks that are truly sensitive and benefit from your involvement.
- Every month, re-assess where you are spending time and how to reallocate tasks again. Ensure that you are growing the talent and responsibilities of your team in a positive way.

If you don't build a foundation of regular delegation when your team is small or when you first start managing it, you will have a very hard time catching up and instilling these practices later when the team becomes busier. Learn the importance of smart delegation.

Chapter 45: Coaching & Development

You create a foundation for growth by constantly gauging where each of your team members are in regards to their own development and providing incremental, actionable feedback.

As you delegate responsibilities and provide tasks for each of your team members to accomplish, you must have a supportive environment. If you want everyone to reach their full potential, there has to be a mantra of, "It is okay to make mistakes." When your team constantly turns to you for advice and you give it, you are not developing their abilities, namely their critical thinking and leadership abilities, which are essential to propelling real growth and innovation.

While we all benefit from the supervision, help, and advice of a boss or mentor, overreliance on others to guide our actions and make decisions limits us from achieving our true heights. There are countless analogies in business, sports, and science. If a human is conditioned to believe the known limits of what he or she can achieve are "x," they will aim to achieve "x," and not even think about 2x or 3x (doubling or tripling the limit). Those who are not told what the limit is, often greatly surpass it. The same holds true for how you develop the members of your organization.

Many managers fear that giving their team too much latitude will lead to serious mistakes being made and goals being missed. Yes, if you suddenly dole out responsibility for some large task without having done so regularly or having first prepared that person, your likelihood of an issue arising is good. But, you can instead encourage an atmosphere of innovation supported by your mentorship that is incremental and keeps most large issues from occurring. Here is a step-by-step approach:

1) Assign tasks and responsibilities that team members can execute at their current level or position.

2) For all tasks that require thinking about a solution or new process, have them think up a solution before they come to you.

3) Discuss their solution first and then work with them on understanding why it is good - when good - or why it wouldn't do well - when bad.

4) Only then should you share your solution with them.

5) If you are unsure as to whether your solution is better than theirs, or if you are both in new waters, create parameters that keep any potential failures limited, such as limiting money or resources devoted to the task, or shortening the time until you review the new solution to limit surprises.

6) Allow them to execute the solution themselves. Sometimes they will fail, sometimes not, but they will learn a lot.

7) Review the results - positive or negative - with them.

Over time, if you are helping to guide and shape their abilities and enhance their confidence, they will be a greater and greater asset, and your involvement shrinks to the big strategic decisions and major problems that arise.

Your goal is to have your team members learn to make decisions and think more critically. This is important to stress because, even at higher managerial levels, too many men and women either can't think for themselves and make the hard decisions, or keep going to their bosses for approval long after they should be able to make the smaller, simpler decisions or insights by themselves. In most of these cases, the blame for this falls directly on that person's former managers for not properly developing their abilities and confidence.

As you do give a person more autonomy, be clear that he or she should keep you informed of larger events, and ask your opinion on more important decisions. That way you still know what is going on within your team and maintain the ability to influence vital factors.

A measure of success as a talent-developing manager lies in accepting that top performers will develop their own styles of work execution, strategy development, and management. Let each member of your team evolve in a way that complements his or her own strengths and natural talents. For example, someone who is very quantitative may use those tools more frequently than you do, and that is great. As long as he or she can arrive at the same quality of solutions and do his or her work well, encourage that sort of development.

Creating Opportunities for Experience

Experience is the primary difference between a junior contributor and a senior contributor; a junior manager and a senior manager. That isn't necessarily a function of time. Just like learning to ride a bicycle, some people pick it up in a couple of tries while others require dozens. That sort of natural skill or leadership ability is wonderful, and we all have some of it through various personal and professional endeavors. But even the most naturally talented people get better as they become more experienced. Experience provides context for decision-making. It provides confidence and it teaches a person how to respond and what resources to marshal for that response.

You should be developing your team by providing them with opportunities to take on more responsibility and / or new responsibilities. If you have armed them with the right information and feedback to succeed, then it is on them to learn from that opportunity and be able to apply its lessons. This is obvious with hard or technical skills, but overlooked more frequently with the soft skills. Regularly review the skills (hard and soft) that are required for a role, assess which of those skills haven't been developed, and create a plan to grow them.

This plan is typically a sequence of:

- Verbal and written training and guidelines on the skill that needs shaping.
- Shadowing / working with others inside or outside of your team who have the skillset and are applying it.
- Parceling out assignments to the person that requires that skillset with a check / backstop by you or someone else on the team to catch errors before it goes external (out of your team to others in the organization or to clients).
- Removing the extra backstop or layer once you have confidence in the person's ability to do it.

The concept of a backstop or check is the significant factor here. Many managers are fearful to give responsibility to a subordinate because they feel that person will mess up a relationship or end up making the team miss the goal. This goes back to the idea of failing constantly. At the end of the day, the more of these opportunities that you can offer your team – starting small, then scaling to medium and large – the more responsibilities they will be able to take on successfully.

Transforming People

Let's say you have what you think of as a "B" player on your team. They can get the work done, but you need to carefully manage his or her planning and review all results as they come from that person, as you inevitably find ways to improve the end product. Sure, that is part of the value and responsibility of a manager, but "A" players on a team are told to "x" and they end up producing "x + 10%," something better than expected. The manager may still have some input, but it is often incremental, with the "A" player working in tandem with the manager on planning and initiatives.

How often can a B-level player be turned into an A-level player? The potential exists much more often than is typically realized. Many managers stay satisfied with "B" players being able to carry out their work and never spend the effort to turn them into "A" players. Or it takes a manager all of his or her time and ability to think about the next strategic goal given to his or her team versus the mid and long-term gains of growing talent.

The Passion Index tool and your constant assessments should help you group your team into a few categories. Building talent is all about supplying your average *and* amazing employees (every person has growth potential, regardless of how good they think they are) with the frameworks, coaching, and tools they need to improve. This improvement will benefit their entire career, even if ultimately not with the same organization, as well as boosting your team's performance.

Here we arrive at a critical point of being a great, successful manager, and not just an average one: Never hold down the potential of one of your team members. Never. Sometimes an average manager who finds they have a diamond on their team, an excellent A-level player, selfishly wants to keep that A-level player forever in the role he or she currently performs, versus giving them more opportunities and actually building the talent. Why? The most common reason is that average managers are afraid that the A-level employees will take their job if someone realizes it is the A-level player that really makes the clock tick. The second-most common reason revolves around a manager thinking that their team will lose its ability to produce if the A-level player departs. Guess what? Most of the time, if an organization has good talent-spotters and talent-builders, someone is going to notice that A-level player, and that average manager will either go away or lose that talent. Or, that A-level player realizes he or she has little opportunity in the organization and leaves to build success elsewhere.

If you truly consider yourself a good manager, you should never be afraid of having A-players on your team. If you can methodically hire and nurture this sort of talent, you know there will be transitions. The transitions can occur when you continue in your own upward trajectory and when you spot opportunities for A-players to advance, within your team or outside of your team.

Maybe you are a manager who loves his or her current job and wouldn't dream of moving elsewhere. You want to be in that exact role forever. First off, there is absolutely nothing wrong with this. Many possibilities exist as to why. Some positions balance that perfect point of an operational position along with a core set of managerial duties. In the armed forces, many excellent sergeants and lieutenants turn down promotion after promotion because they like being where the action is; they can be there to shape what happens in real-time. Or maybe the next step up in your career means sacrificing elements of your personal or family life that you don't want to sacrifice.

The good manager, however, in such a role, will still build the talent on their team! That manager isn't fearful of losing his or her position. Instead, they foster a reputation for producing high quality talent that goes on to make large contributions elsewhere.

Gain a reputation for helping people develop and advance their careers and you will have an abundance of talented people who wish to work with you.

Chapter 46: Becoming a Manager of Managers

Many new managers get into a role without any sort of seasoning or experience operating at that particular level. (This can be your first management responsibility, or you may be bumped up from managing 10 people to 200.) Some of these managers do great when they are thrown into the fire, some don't. Especially if you have suffered through the curve of building this experience, don't do it to your team. Prepare those who wish to become managers.

As all of Part Two in the book stresses, the key principles in being a successful manager are developing strategy and building teams. Not everyone wants to become a manager. Of those who do, some will wish to do the sort of role that you currently hold, while others may wish to become managers in their individual functions, such as one of your salespeople wishing to manage a team of salespeople in the future. This is relevant as frequently managers focus on developing the traits of what they consider their #2 or #3 person in the team for their own role and spend much less time with others who have the desire and potential. But that is an error, as it takes many types of managers with different talents and specializations to operate at larger levels.

As you think about developing your team, look to your top people - in any area - and consider whether they hold the potential to be great managers. Ask yourself if they:

- Want to become managers.
- Display an ability to think strategically, understand the strategy of team, and contribute to that strategy.

- Have excellent peer management skills.
- Take ownership for their actions and the actions of others in the same way you do.

Some candidates may have all of the above traits, except for the desire to actually be a manager. Often, this is a fear of failure or a hesitation to take on certain duties they don't enjoy. Sometimes it is a lack of comprehension on what it truly means to be a manager. It is your job in your evaluations and discussions with that person to figure out whether he or she truly understands the role and doesn't want it, or just thinks that he or she doesn't want it.

Once you identify the people that display the above traits, give them the opportunities to build experience in the manager's domain: strategy development and team building.

Strategy Development

The ability to create strategy is the easier one of the two areas to cultivate because much of it can be done on paper or through discussion, at least initially. Just as you give your team smaller opportunities to come up with tactics and ideas, ensure that you:

- Take great pains to educate them on the team's strategy and how it fits into the organization's strategy.
- Teach them how to assess strategies within the team and in other competitors and industries.
- Give them research projects that require them to create strategies for new initiatives you are given.

For those people on your team who have proven themselves over and over again, you can give them the responsibility to execute parts of the existing or new strategy that they have helped shape.

Team Building

Team building consists of hiring people, managing their activities, and developing their talents. You can provide opportunities to do all three.

Use the hiring process when you are building your team to give experience to potential managers. Not only does that help you in your decision-making process for new hires, but it educates your team members in a very deep way. Do you really need help in making hiring decisions? Not necessarily and not all the time. Could those hours your potential managers spend be instead utilized doing other work? Of course. But this is a key skill that a manager must develop, and it gives you additional sets of thoughts on candidates. To train your potential members effectively means including them to the point that they grasp the full scope of the process: crafting a job posting, resume screening, and conducting interviews. You don't ever have to make them solely responsible for any element; instead, you can give them the same work you are doing and then speak with them after they have concluded.

Have these individuals conduct their own one-on-one interviews by phone and in-person, as well as have them sit in on the sessions where you are interviewing a candidate. Following the interview, make sure to ask them their impressions on the candidate, and any different approaches and questions that could have been asked. Finally, share your own impressions and discuss them.

Opportunities to manage people carry more risk. But if you want to develop effective managers within your own team, you must offer those opportunities. First, give team members peer management opportunities (on specific projects or by having them dole out tasks to the team). From there, incrementally progress to assigning more formal responsibilities to manage one person's workload and day-to-day tasks. For example, let's say you have a potential manager named Stewart. Start Stewart on the path to becoming a manager by giving him a few management responsibilities and informing his peers of the upcoming transition. For example, you might say: "Stacy, all of your assignments are going to come from Stewart for the next month." On a weekly or biweekly basis, you check in with Stewart and challenge him on what he is doing in regards to managing Stacy and how he is doing it.

With Stacy, ensure that you have spoken with her beforehand, so she doesn't feel this is a negative action being taken against her, and then check in periodically to get feedback on how she thinks Stewart is doing. You can then relay that information to Stewart. For example, "Stewart, the issue seems to be that you are trying to show Stacy the process too quickly, and she's not understanding it because you skip from step 1 to step 8." Or, "Stewart, you are not being patient enough with Stacy when she makes mistakes and are not explaining to her what she did wrong and giving her different possible solutions." Will Stewart make some mistakes with Stacy? Of course, but you are still there overseeing everything. If your oversight is sufficient, Stewart will come out with a lot of experience. You can rotate Stewart in different areas of responsibility, assign him to more people, or scale back your oversight and give him more autonomy. There are plenty of ways that allow him to continue to develop. The biggest test is that your potential manager can make decisions in a methodical manner, and that he or she is proving that they do well in managing others.

One of the hardest things for a manager to do is to let go, but just as you have to do this with all of your team members, you must allow potential managers even more latitude to flourish. At some point, as your team grows, your responsibilities grow. You may receive a promotion or you may now have an opportunity for a potential manager elsewhere in the organization. When this is the case, make the person you have been gradually developing into a formal manager. When that day arrives, or if you are already there, you must give any managers that you manage their true autonomy. Don't hover around their direct reports or make all of their decisions for them. That disempowers your manager and doesn't allow them to execute to their true potential. Set them up to do well on their own merits in the same way you always wish or wished you had been set up to succeed.

If you can successfully become a manager not only to contributors, but to managers underneath you, you have passed the final hurdles in succeeding big professionally. The sky will be your limit.

Chapter 47: A Final Note

Learn to think strategically and manage well, and you will truly give yourself unbounded opportunities. Great managers in the peak of their careers don't do it for the money. Almost all have made more than enough to keep them comfortable for the rest of their lives, or they simply don't care about money. They continue to manage in their organizations in part because of their love for what they do, and in part because their decisions have such large, often lasting, impacts. Each day brings its own challenges, as well as its own rewards, but that is what keeps life so interesting.

One of my favorite times during the day is about 10AM when my team and I are working full tilt. There is a great energy in the office. I hear ten different conversations going on about different projects we have in motion. Once in a while, one of them hops into my office with a brief question, but the people I've hired are really smart, really good team-players. I work with them on strategy and personal development, but, at the end of the day, it is this culture of open responsibility and communication that helps us achieve our strong results. As I feel this energy, I smile for a bit, roll up my sleeves, and dive in again.

Part Three: My Journey Thus Far

What follows is a brief autobiography. Its point is to frame some of my thinking for you and to serve, hopefully, as an inspiration to always push the envelope. This autobiography isn't meant to be complete and thorough. It is cherry-picked to what I think are some of the more defining points in my life. You will find its tone more serious than uplifting as it focuses more on the trials and learning experiences. Why highlight the trials? To be more authentic. I've read too many books that talk about all of the great things a businessperson has accomplished, with little mention of all of the failures and lessons learned to get to the successes. Successes are easy to talk about and we often forget about the hard work that was necessary to get there.

A grittier story that does go into the failures better explains the forces that have shaped my experience and gotten me to where I am today. This was the hardest section to write because it reveals so much about myself and my faults. I don't like talking about myself in great detail, and this book is not meant to be an autobiography. For all of those reasons, I have placed this section last in the book and kept it short.

There are countless things I look to and say, "I wish I had done that differently," or, "I wish I had handled that differently." I feel as if I've made many mistakes - professionally and personally - in the last ten years. This balances against successes professionally, financially, and personally. I wake up every day full of energy, wanting to push the limits of what I can achieve. Outside of the professional-focused side of me, I spend my free time running (I've discovered mud runs recently) and in other forms of exercise, cooking, a good book, and enjoying those always-too-short perfect moments spent having fun and relaxing with family and friends.

But let's start at the beginning. I've been a planner and a dreamer for as long as I can remember. If you asked the 17-year-old me what I wanted to be by the age of 30, I would have told you, "A billionaire who runs his own companies and is known as an innovator, has been to space, has a sweet loft somewhere, and travels around the world." (I know, pretty much Elon Musk.) I'm not complaining about where I am now, but life is certainly different from what I imagined it would be.

Peeking into the basement of my parents' home, you would find one of the building blocks of my education. My father is an avid reader; by the time I could read, he had assembled an entire room of books on all manner of subjects: philosophy, medicine, business management, biographies on famous leaders, investing, cooking, and science fiction (one of my favorite genres to this day). As a child and teenager, I devoured every book in that room, adding many more of my own.

I grew up in Illinois, attending middle and high school in Rockford. My upbringing was typical in many ways; a working middle-class family where, at times, money was tight, but always enough to put food on the table.

My mother and grandmother have always inspired me with their amazing work ethics. My grandmother never went past a high school education, yet she has more common sense than almost anyone I've ever met. Now in her mid-seventies, she can still work harder than most people half her age. She moved near us when I was born, and after a few years was employed as a manager in an Italian deli. When she wasn't working twelve hours in the deli, she lived with the store's owners, helping to raise their many children. My grandmother has attempted to live with us on three separate occasions, but she goes back to work every time after a few weeks because she just can't sit around doing nothing; she loves being productive. My mother shares this same philosophy, working long hours as a research chemist when she is not pursuing advanced skills in yoga. She also happens to be an amazingly talented artist, a trait that seems to have skipped a generation.

My father has always been an inspiration, as well as an example, on the ups and downs of life. Originally educated as a mechanical engineer, he decided in his early 20s that working for others wouldn't allow him the personal freedom and financial rewards of owning his own company. Over the course of his life, he has built three, separate, multi-million dollar businesses in the construction and automotive industries. Tragically, however, he has lost those three businesses, one in an economic downturn and two from bad business partners. Not having married and had children until he was almost forty years old, he is now at retirement age. He still has a knack for making enough money independently to keep my family getting by. His support for me has been ever-constant in whatever I have pursued. His life experiences, especially the failures, together with my own, have certainly shaped the way I think about the world.

The other constant in my life from the age of four through college was martial arts. In particular, Won Sun Jung, a grandmaster in Tae Kwon Do & Hapkido. Jung came from South Korea, where he had been a two-time national Tae Kwon Do champion. He arrived in the U.S. in the 1970s with little but his martial arts skills and many dreams. By the time I met him in 1997, he had trained hundreds of black belts, ran 13 satellite schools through his advanced students, and was a multimillionaire. Won Son Jung's philosophy was to give a lot of latitude and trust to his senior students, really throwing them in the deep-end with responsibilities, giving them more and more as they proved themselves. By the age of 14, I taught the children's classes five days a week, while attending the adult classes later in the evenings. Those lessons in teaching and leadership have been priceless. Won Son Jung's achievements as a self-made man greatly influenced my own desires to work hard and reach my dreams.

By the time I got to high school, between the books I had read on great organizations, my father, and Won Sun Jung, I had a strong notion that I wanted to be an entrepreneur. I started keeping a little notebook with all of the ideas I had; six or seven ideas a day, all of which seemed absolutely brilliant as I scribbled them down. Business concepts, business names, quotes I liked, everything went into that little book.

In the summer before my junior year of high school, a friend and I joined together and started planning a charity. Our high school had a requirement of 90 hours of community service per year, and since he and I were both entrepreneurial, we figured why do community service for others, when instead we could create our own charity and be in charge? It would also look good when we applied to colleges. Win-win concept all around. We called it "United Charities," thinking it sounded like a good, big official name. United Charities' core purpose was to select one cause every year for which we raised money.

He and I did everything required to start an organization. We created a logo and website, and incorporated and applied for non-profit status, all before we actually had a business plan. (No one had yet taught us that the "build it and they will come" philosophy doesn't work very often...) When all of that had been completed, and we were hundreds of dollars in the red from our personal savings, we actually came up with the business plan for *how* to raise money. It wasn't brilliant or original. We figured going door-to-door would be a fast and easy way to get in front of people who could - and hopefully would - donate a few dollars. The money would accumulate with every house and we would be successful overnight.

It turned out to be a little harder than we thought. Actually, much harder. This kind of experience is where you first learn how to create and refine a sales pitch. Weather also became an obstacle, as we started going door-to-door in late September, when temperatures had already dropped into the low 40s.

The first ten houses we visited went something like this:

(Door opens.)

Us: "Hi! We are United Charities! We are raising money for HIV awareness. Could you donate a dollar?"

Them: "Who? United Charities? Is that part of United Way? We already donate to other charities. (Skeptical look at the two teenagers on their doorstep.) No thanks."

(Door closes.)

'Okay,' we thought. 'This wasn't going to be a cakewalk....'

At the end of a long, cold afternoon, we had collected $4.30. I remember that total very clearly, as we laughed - the kind of laugh you make when you don't want to cry - that it was less than one of us would have made for an hour's work at a minimum wage job. And this was for charity too. A great pair of businessmen we were making out to be.

Dinner and a hot chocolate later, we were back to planning. This time we started thinking about what had gone wrong and what we could improve. We figured our neighborhood selection was good, we just didn't have a good enough message and pitch. Late that evening, we had our epiphany, inspired by the candy bars students often sell to make money for school trips: We would provide a tangible item that people could buy, with the profits going to our charitable cause. The candy bar market seemed a little saturated, so we started visiting a number of stores, trying to find items that would have enough margin to sell. The bigger the margin, we thought, the less of it we would need to reach our goals. A visit to a thrift store was in order. There we found nice-looking candles and potpourri that looked like those that cost $5 or $10, but were just $0.99 each. Bingo.

The next day after school, we picked a new neighborhood and began again. My friend carried one candle, and I held a bag of potpourri. After about twenty houses, we had sold two candles, making $10. Better than day one but, at this rate, we would be visiting half the city to raise any major money.

Every evening, we would evaluate our results and try to improve on them. I didn't realize it then, but the skill of constantly trying to improve the status quo would be a key lesson for me later on. Our next major breakthrough happened when we made official looking name-tags to pin on our jackets, printed name cards with a website, and created good-looking boxes to carry our candles and potpourri. We had developed an official-looking brand.

At our peak, with smiles, a good greeting and message, professional signage and nice items for sale, we were getting about one house in eight to make a donation.

United Charities was never a large success, or even a medium one. It unraveled as we got busy in the winter of our senior year in high school with college applications; it died completely as we enjoyed those final few months of the senior year, where you feel like you are on top of the world. The lessons learned, however, about what it takes to start a business, the sales process, brand identity, and knowing your customer, those remained.

I also wanted to make money for myself. Outside of school and martial arts (Teaching martial arts didn't pay anything. My martial arts master understood the value of cheap labor at the time infinitely more than I did...) I did gardening work for neighbors, helped start a gaming business for teens, and also worked at a local fast-food restaurant. I've never been above doing any type of work that is assigned to me when I'm the one that needs to do it, and working at a fast food restaurant sure taught me that lesson well. My job for the first two months was washing dishes, wading through seemingly endless sinks of greasy, burned, and smelly pots, pans, and dishes. I'm still proud of the fact that I actually re-organized and bettered the system for washing these items, getting the owner to install a new drying system and reducing the time to wash all of the dishes (properly) to about half of what it had taken the previous dishwasher.

Between martial arts, school, and work, time flew and I graduated high school with a healthy amount of dollars that I'd made from my various endeavors, and an eagerness to make my stamp on the world.

I was accepted to a number of colleges and decided to go the University of Chicago. I would like to say I made the decision after a spring visit (during which I sat in on a five-person class discussing the history of the Roman Empire), but that wouldn't be the whole truth. I certainly appreciated the university visit, but it was a combination of an (older) girlfriend who was in Chicago already, an introduction to a martial arts school in the city, and Chicago itself that all swayed my decision.

Deciding to attend the University of Chicago (short-handedly known as The U of C or UChicago) is a decision I have never regretted. The more time that has passed since my graduation, the more I appreciate the special place that the University of Chicago was (and is) and how much I learned and enjoyed my time there; the professors, the knowledge, the friends.

UChicago in 2004 was not a hotbed of entrepreneurial or even business-minded students. The school has a long-standing reputation for serious academic work, with many Nobel Prize winners among its faculty. During the 2004 to 2008 period I was there, there were no undergraduate courses in anything business-related. If someone was interested in being an entrepreneur, consultant, investment banker, or trader, majoring in economics was the closest he or she could get, paired with a few business school classes at the adjacent campus. (Though looking back, I've realized how valuable a liberal arts education can be on giving you a broader perspective on the world.) I started with a goal of being an economics major. There were a few business clubs on campus, and I quickly joined one known as The ILC. The ILC exists to this day, focused on bringing together students interested in entrepreneurship, consulting, investing, and technology. I made many friends from The ILC; friends with whom I would spend most of my time during college.

I participated in a couple of student start-ups during my first six months on campus, while I looked about for interesting business opportunities of my own. My notebook of business ideas continued to fill up, day after day. Early in the spring of 2005, a group of friends and I were sitting around eating lunch when we came up with the idea for Nodorm. Nodorm was a business meant to help students who were looking for housing after their first year of college in dorms find apartments of their own. One of six "co-founders," as we liked to call ourselves, I was the second-in-command behind a senior classman for a month, until he received an offer to study abroad. I took the title of CEO of Nodorm, leading two programmers and another two classmates serving in operational and sales roles.

As a website service, Nodorm wasn't hard to build. We had two ace programmers who pretty quickly created an apartment listing service. (They were good enough to be scouted to work for Amazon upon graduation.) Our bigger challenge was the fact that we had two sets of customers. One set was apartment landlords, who we wanted payment from to list their apartments on our website. Students were the second set of customers; students who we had to make not only aware of the Nodorm website, but trust us enough to use it. These types of business models are difficult, but we didn't know any better, so we just dove in.

Nodorm started out well. Students who had never rented before wanted the help, and landlords had plenty of apartments they wanted to fill. A single month's rent is a lot of money; multiply that by dozens of units and the landlords had a lot of financial incentive to get their places rented as quickly as possible. My partners and I secured a visit with the largest landlord in Hyde Park at the time (the neighborhood around the University of Chicago). We had planned a good sales pitch: as students, we knew how to market to our fellow students, and therefore we could increase their rented units. The landlord liked the idea enough that he wrote us a check for a little over $5,000. That was the biggest sale I had ever made up to that point in my career. The landlord figured we could easily help him more quickly rent the additional ten units it would take for him break-even, and he had a lot of upside from there.

Check in hand, we had to start actually marketing to students. We studied what other people were doing, and we began a huge print and viral campaign. Many an evening were spent chalking in front of student dorms, hanging posters, showing up at events and parties, handing out cards… on and on. It worked, and students at UChicago started using the Nodorm website as we gained almost every major landlord in Hyde Park as a client. Because most students sorted their housing situations between March and May of every year, by the time my freshman year ended, we had some money in the bank and a calm summer to look forward to.

That summer I decided to stay and live in Chicago, in Hyde Park, to pursue other business ventures. What I was really struck by was a lack of focus and delusions of grandeur from my success at Nodorm. I planned or started three or four additional businesses during that summer, including a website hosting service, figuring that every single one would be a vast success and I would be rolling in riches in short order. I figured everything I touched would turn to gold. I ended up making about $12,000 from my little endeavors over the summer, but the months quickly passed, and before too long, my sophomore year began.

In the first few weeks of my second year, I decided to change my major from economics to political science. I would like to tell you that I switched because political science captivated and amazed me and broadened my mind with an awareness of how the world worked, but that was to be an unexpected plus later. My main reason at the time was primarily "economical." (Bad pun, I know, I'm full of them.) Economics classes required weekly problem-set submissions that required a lot of regular hours, and it was time I just didn't feel I had. Nodorm was ramping up again with bigger plans, and I was juggling a number of other start-up business ideas on top of it. Political science classes typically had only two papers due during each trimester, based on books we were assigned to read and discuss in-class. I never had difficulty writing and loved reading. I figured I could crank out a ten-page paper in a single evening-late night combination, saving me time to focus on my entrepreneurial activities.

The first semester of my second year started with growth for Nodorm. We decided to expand the company to other major colleges in Chicago, including DePaul, Loyola, UIC, and Northwestern. Almost every night, the Nodorm crew would head out to one of those colleges to execute our guerilla-style marketing. It was exhilarating watching our website traffic grow and to see people enjoying the service but, drunk on the fumes of my (relative) success and realizing Nodorm was a really niche business, my mind continued to race late at night, thinking of new opportunities.

These were the days of Facebook when Facebook was still a

college phenomenon, growing and sweeping across the country. Together with Myspace, social networks were the hot thing, and my mind constantly drifted to the idea of how I could create my own version. Good social networks could scale quickly and were receiving serious interest from investors around the world. On the other hand, Facebook didn't make any money at the time, and everyone talked about the dangers and pitfalls of companies that had no revenue stream. I racked my brain and one winter night, the idea for Collectica was born.

Collectica combined a social network with an auction platform. The core idea was to create a space dedicated to collectors (of all things, from comics to stamps to art) who wanted to share their collections with their peers, and also to sell them in a curated environment. The day after I came up with the initial concept, I called on two of my co-founders in Nodorm and started to weave the story of Collectica together.

One incredible resource we had available to us was the University of Chicago's entrepreneurship program, known in shorthand as the "Polsky Center." The Polsky Center offered support – financial and mentorship – to would-be entrepreneurs in the university system; primarily for those in the graduate school of business, but also accessible to undergraduates. Its core asset at the time was the New Venture Challenge, a competition where teams could enter business plans and ultimately pitch their ideas to actual venture capital investors. Best of all, it had a 10-week class that taught you everything about writing a business plan and the various elements of starting and running a company. I had actually participated in the competition as a junior team member with the previous year's winner, PrepMe, founded by a good friend of mine.

The entire competition was an invaluable learning experience. I was paired not only with senior faculty advisors, but also connected with former participants of the competition who were now successful businessmen and businesswomen in their own right. Over a series of months, I learned every element of creating and building an organization, from finance, to marketing, to operations, to hiring and scaling for growth. Not to mention public speaking. I was lucky that my overconfidence or smugness balanced against a real desire to learn from others. It was likely this latter trait that resonated most with everyone who helped me. Because I truly valued the things I was learning, and loved learning them, these fine people didn't mind mentoring me.

Week after week, we built the business plan for Collectica and, more than that, actually built the business itself. I didn't want to simply have a business plan; I wanted Collectica to be the next big social network. Through the school and contacts, we assembled a team of some pretty senior people and began mocking out the website, soliciting feedback from potential users / customers, and making real headway in establishing Collectica as a viable business.

This actual momentum translated into Collectica getting through the 10-week class, then into the semi-finals of the competition, and then, into the finals. I still remember my last sentence of the presentation. It went something like this: "This is a real company with real momentum. Tonight, whether we win or lose, we are driving out to a convention in Washington D.C. where we will be promoting Collectica to collectors." Collectica didn't win the competition outright. We actually shared first place with a company you may have heard of if you have ever ordered restaurant delivery: GrubHub (a now publically-traded, highly successful endeavor).

With Collectica's tie for first-place, we were able to raise a round of money from angel investors and build a great team. The core of the team was a brilliant website developer – who I'm happy to say co-owns a highly successful technology consulting firm these days – surrounded by several alumnae of the university, and a group of students with unbounded energy and determination. Fully committed, I decided to take a leave of absence from college, since I was starting to fail my classes anyway.

There is nothing like owning your own company to make you want to learn every element of running one. Collectica was my first "real" career. It served as the foundation for many of the lessons I learned and share with you in this book.

For over a year, Collectica was my life. We were building the website, marketing to collectors virtually and in-person with travel across the country, and really trying to grow something special. It had the benefits of the ability to scale quickly combined with many potential sources of revenue from collectors, dealers, and vendors. The core of Collectica never changed, but we made hundreds – probably thousands – of incremental tweaks as we hit roadblocks. Businesses rarely end up looking like the original business plan. Eventually we started to find real traction by seeking to partner with various collector's associations through the country. We were on our way to success, slowly and with bumps, but surely.

Three key developments ultimately combined to doom Collectica. One was a result of my hubris. We felt we were doing so well that we could afford to replace the primary angel investor, who had his own ideas about the company's directions, with another investor. The second development was a loss of a major partnership with one of the largest collector's associations that would have driven guaranteed revenue to the company. The deal was signed on a Saturday and, two days later, annulled by internal turmoil in the association. Development one or two alone wouldn't have been catastrophic. The investor market was hot and we felt we could raise more money; the partnership was simply stalled as we restarted the relationship. But development number three occurred in the fall of 2007: The beginning of the financial upheaval in the U.S. and across the world. In the span of a three-month period, all investor money dried up as everyone panicked, and suddenly Collectica didn't have any money left in the bank, while it had many bills and people to pay.

I didn't sleep much in those months, constantly scrambling to find a way out of the crisis. It wasn't to be. The reality was that we had partners with families or who wanted to start families. We all needed money to live; we couldn't shoestring it, despite a desire to continue forward. In the end, we probably kept going for too long and I burned too many bridges trying to keep it going. But failure is a difficult pill to swallow.

Thus, in December 2007, we decided to close Collectica down; its last days were in January of 2008. The loss of Collectica almost destroyed me. It cost me many friends, many mentors, my savings, and almost all of my confidence. I had taken a leave of absence from school, so I wasn't enrolled anywhere either. Had it not been for my amazing girlfriend at the time, who kept faith in me, I would have stayed off the rails for a much longer period. You often take for granted the love and support of friends and family; it isn't until you realize how much they are there for you that you learn to truly appreciate them.

With Collectica gone, I applied to end my leave of absence and was accepted back to the U of C in early 2008. I had only two things going for me at that point: My girlfriend and finishing my degree. It was really the first time I had focused on school, and I dove in as a way to distract me from my depression. It was during these months that I began engaging with political science and learning about how the world worked on many different levels politically, socially, and economically. I had gained some weight during this entire period - never fat, but as my mother likes to say, my cheeks in my graduation picture were really round - so I began exercising when I could again.

In August of 2008, I finished my final class and prepared to graduate with a degree in political science. With graduation looming, I still didn't know what I wanted to do, but allergic to the idea of a "conventional" job, I began doing affiliate marketing and arbitrage with digital marketing efforts to make some money. I also partnered with a senior marketer to start consulting with various companies around the country who were seeking to apply digital marketing strategies to their brick and mortar businesses, ultimately working with a sharp group of people in these efforts. I tinkered around with many business ideas, as well as diving deeper into the world of investing.

While I learned much during the first 18 months out of college, I realized that being a maverick and a consultant, or a maverick consultant, wasn't going to help me make it big. I had made some money and learned a lot about different types of industries and operations, but I wasn't actually helping to grow something, nor able to claim true pride of ownership. I reflected that while I had created a number of smaller business opportunities, none of them had scaled in size (or would scale) in a way I thought would bring large success. The hole I felt was in my understanding of how companies grew from small to large, and while it wasn't a great time to go anywhere fast with the recession in full swing, I realized I needed to participate in and experience that sort of growth and environment first-hand.

Thus, I began a formal job hunt process. The year 2010 was not a great time to be hunting for positions, with companies still sticking to very conservative hiring practices as no one knew whether the economic recession would continue down into an economic depression. Searching for a full-time position during this rocky period motivated me to learn all that I could about the best ways to apply to jobs and stand out from other candidates. Despite all of that, it was still hard. The few jobs that had openings during this time each received hundreds of applicants. I nearly took worse jobs (in terms of pay or opportunity) a few times, but kept holding off, waiting for the right fit. Then, the opportunity at Timberline Knolls came along.

The job ad for Timberline Knolls was written very oddly.

Despite it being a marketing analysis and operations position inside what was already a multi-million dollar company, the headline and body of the job posting went along the lines of: An entrepreneurial company in the healthcare industry, backed by large investors, is growing fast and wants to find a go-getter with experience in marketing and analysis. No actual mention of Timberline Knolls or that it was specifically part of the behavioral healthcare industry. The ad, however, caught my eye as it stood out from everything else. I applied to it as I had with all of my other positions, with a great deal of care and investment.

I really put a great deal of energy into the process. As soon as I knew what the company was, I learned as much as I could about the behavioral healthcare industry and how I could apply my skillsets to it. By the time I got to in-person interviews, I had dug through the website, researched the competitors, noted a few of the company's deficiencies, as well as some opportunities, and gained a passing familiarity with behavioral healthcare marketing, something I had never even thought of prior to that job ad. Some weeks later, I received an offer and accepted. It's funny how life works that way. You rarely end up doing what you first envision. Behavioral healthcare marketing? Certainly not something I had ever thought of seriously before.

What appealed to me most about Timberline Knolls, and what ultimately sold me on it, was its majority investor and CEO, James, who was a serial entrepreneur. This was a company that, unlike most at the time, was actually rapidly growing through the recession. James knew how to create a brand, a strategy, and build a team of smart people to grow a company.

For two years I worked and learned not only the marketing side of behavioral health, but many of its operational facets as well, courtesy of the great people with whom I interacted. I felt like I was part of something that was special, and it felt good to truly regain my confidence in the ability to contribute to the strategy and growth of such an organization. I had a couple of key mentors in Zach, Jan, and James, all of whom taught me not only the mechanics of the business, but also a better appreciation for the importance of interpersonal relationships and communication.

In 2012, I had the opportunity to live in China for six months. James was generously flexible and gave the okay for me to work remotely. As most of my tasks were done via computer, I worked during normal business hours, took a break in the early evening, and made international calls from 9pm to 1am Shanghai time, which corresponded to early and mid-day in the U.S. It was a small trade-off to allow me to keep working and earning money while living in such a different environment.

China holds a very special place in my memory. I lived in Shanghai, which is best described as Chicago or New York in the 1930s - vast, alive, humming with energy. You can find absolutely everything in Shanghai from all around the world, in addition to countless things unique to China. I had a true insider's tour, visiting not only the internationally known tourist areas, but many locations revered by the Chinese that are little known outside of the country. One of my favorite memories is sitting among huge bamboo stands like those in the movie, *Crouching Tiger, Hidden Dragon*, listening to the wind rustle through the forest, while eating local roasted nuts. I regret that I have not kept up my knowledge of Mandarin in the years since my return.

In my last few months in China, I had a call with James, the CEO, during which he told me that he had sold the Timberline Knolls to a company called Acadia Healthcare. He assured me he had put in a good word for me and that my future with Timberline Knolls would be secure, with the deal closing in the fall of 2012. I couldn't do much from China except to trust his word and see how the cards would unfold.

Early in 2013, I had been back in the States for some time. Acadia Healthcare had taken a hands-off approach for the first months of its ownership of Timberline Knolls and life hadn't really changed much. As I evaluated my next steps, I felt like I had reached a plateau at Timberline Knolls, and I had begun exploring other options with other companies, as well as thinking of starting a venture of my own again. But other forces began to work. As I've said, Timberline Knolls was (and continues to be) something special. Acadia hadn't owned this type of facility before, and its COO, Ron, decided to pay some visits to the facility. Ron wanted to better understand who and what made up the seemingly "secret sauce" behind Timberline Knolls' success and set up meetings with the senior staff.

I'm pretty sure I barely made the cut-off for "senior staff," but the work we had been doing in online marketing and brand development must have caught his eye enough to figure he might as well meet with some of the marketing folks. It was different from how Acadia had approached marketing in the past. I flew to

Acadia's headquarters, participated in the presentation and then heard nothing from Ron for some time.

Then, one day, I was told, "Ron is coming to Timberline Knolls again, and he wants to meet with you for 30 minutes." Through a blend of cockiness and naiveté, I really didn't fully understand the significance or opportunity of a full 30-minute meeting with Ron. I didn't grasp his seniority in the industry, his vast successes to date, or his ability to easily vault me into a much greater point in my career.

Lucky for me (and this is where that quote from the beginning of the book comes in), I always prepare for these sorts of meetings, and I at least realized it was *an* opportunity.

I guess I did okay enough at explaining what I did and why it worked, as Ron came back some weeks later and offered me the VP of Marketing position at Acadia, overseeing consumer marketing for the entire company. I don't want you to think it was only what I said to Ron that created the opportunity. One's reputation (read: what other people say about you) matters. The feedback Ron received on me from Timberline Knolls' senior staff, including James and Jan, tipped the scales, I'm more than sure.

Jan has been an amazing mentor and constant supporter. Jan held senior executive positions in large healthcare companies before my parents even met. She epitomizes two key values of a strong manager, ones you hear me repeat throughout this book: strategy and team-building. Ron's focus on identifying, cultivating, and empowering people has driven him to huge success. His success has been a huge reinforcement of my own philosophies, and his support has been constant.

To me, the number of people a great manager has successfully coached and trained in his or her professional career marks greatness. By that standard, Ron and Jan have few peers. Find a couple of Rons and Jans in your career to be your mentors, and you will do well.

As of this book's publication date in 2015, I've held the VP of Marketing position at Acadia for two years. During that time, the company has quintupled in size. I oversee a team of truly talented men and women who, together, make magical things happen. I have many amazing mentors and I'm constantly learning more as I, in turn, apply what I have already learned in my work and in leading others.

I'm not and I never shall be perfect. Instead, I've learned how to create and channel smaller failures into positive momentum, together with learning the art of managing expectations. With the ups and downs professionally, there have been similar ups and downs personally. But that's a story for another time.

To date, I've had the benefit of working for my own start-ups, consulting to many types of industries, as well as being a part of a multi-billion dollar company; this book is the distillation of all of the valuable lessons I have absorbed along the way. The team at Acadia is my current test environment for strategies and developing talent. May they have your deepest of sympathies.

My journey is not yet complete, and it won't be for a long time if I have anything to say (and do) about it. The me from high school could never have predicted the me of today. I'll keep failing and I'll keep succeeding. And if my failures end up being smaller than my successes, I'll do alright. In fact, I'll do better than alright and continue to succeed big professionally. I hope you do too.

Best wishes,

- Michael Drake

Made in the USA
Charleston, SC
10 June 2015